Gospel Light's

EARLY CHILD-HOOD SMART PAGES

By **Sheryl Haystead**

The complete resource for teacher training and recruiting

Gospel Light

HOW TO MAKE CLEAN COPIES FROM THIS BOOK

You may make copies of portions of this book with a clean conscience if

• you (or someone in your organization) are the original purchaser;

• you are using the copies you make for a noncommercial purpose (such as teaching or promoting your ministry) within your church or organization;

• you follow the instructions provided in this book.

However, it is ILLEGAL for you to make copies if

• you are using the material to promote, advertise or sell a product or service other than for ministry fund-raising;

• you are using the material in or on a product for sale; or

• you or your organization are not the original purchaser of this book.

By following these guidelines you help us keep our products affordable.

Thank you,

Gospel Light

NOTE

EDITORIAL STAFF

Founder, Henrietta Mears • **Publisher Emeritus,** William T. Greig • **Publisher, Children's Curriculum and Resources,** Lynnette Pennings, M.A. • **Senior Consulting Publisher,** Dr. Elmer L. Towns • **Managing Editor,** Sheryl Haystead • **Senior Consulting Editor,** Wesley Haystead, M.S.Ed. • **Senior Editor, Biblical and Theological Issues,** Bayard Taylor, M.Div. • **Editorial Team,** Deborah Barber, Mary Gross • **Contributing Editors,** Candy Baylis, Debbie Broyles, Cindy Donohue, Willamae Myers, Barbara Platt, Benjamin Unseth • **Senior Designer,** Carolyn Thomas

Contents

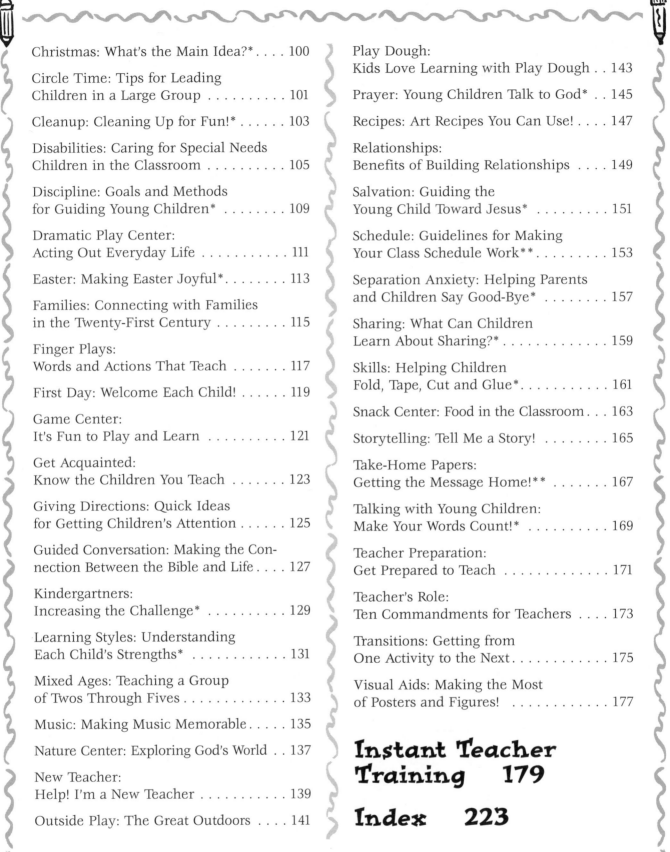

*These articles are recommended for use in parent education classes.

**If your church does not use Gospel Light curriculum, modify these articles to reflect your curriculum.

How to Make a Difference in the Lives of Young Children

If the teachers in your church are like most teachers, they want to feel like they're making a significant difference in the lives of the young children they teach and care for. As busy people choose whether or not to be involved in ministry to children, they want to know that their time will be well spent. Sometimes, however, either from a lack of awareness or from misguided priorities, a church misses the opportunity to effectively nurture young children. Instead of creating purposeful programs that help young children begin to build a lifelong foundation of faith, a minimum of Christian Education is given. Teachers want to feel they are doing more than baby-sitting or filling time.

The goal of this book is to help you focus your church's early childhood programs for significant benefits and results in the Christian growth of preschoolers. The development of a quality early childhood Christian education ministry starts with careful consideration of this key question: What are the ways in which young children learn and grow in their understanding of who God is and how His Word gives direction for everyday life?

The Big Picture of Learning

Examine your ideas about learning. It's generally assumed that learning follows four steps:

1. Gain new information.

2. Come to understand the meaning of the new information.

3. Develop attitudes and beliefs about that meaning.

4. Put the information into practice.

With young children, however, a great deal of learning occurs almost in reverse:

1. Experience something that is true.

2. Accept that experience as true.

3. Repeat the experience often enough so that the truth begins to be understood.

4. Hear words that describe that truth, giving the truth a new richness and resulting in additional understanding.

As this cycle repeats itself over and over, a child's learning and understanding grow in significant ways.

This cycle of learning applies to education in all areas of life, including Christian education. Therefore, an effective early childhood ministry gives teachers the tools to help children learn through everyday experiences coupled with the words of Bible truth. Such a ministry will truly make a difference in the spiritual nurture of children.

The Hallmark of Christian Education

The hallmark of Christian education for preschoolers is active play experiences that engage each child with loving Christian adults. Play is not only the way the young child learns about objects, people and relationships; but it is also the best way for a young child to learn about God and His love. The Christian faith we share with children must be more than mere words or information. It is not enough for the young child to hear God's Word or even to memorize it. The child must live it. A child is not yet able to listen to explanations about the concepts and beliefs of Christian faith: the child must play with materials. In order to learn effectively, the child uses all of his or her senses—seeing, touching, tasting, smelling and hearing.

Therefore, we can best help children learn Bible truths by providing active play experiences that a teacher connects to Bible stories and verses through comments and questions. As teachers use words to describe ways children are putting God's Word into action, the child's play takes on the qualities of Bible learning. The combination of words and actions, frequently repeated, expands and clarifies the child's thinking. This kind of active learning cannot be rushed. It takes time! Early childhood programs that allow for significant active learning time provide the most benefit to young children.

You can help others in your church (teachers, parents, church staff) understand these key principles of learning and the importance of young children in a church's view of ministry. Distribute copies of "How Young Children Learn" (pp. 7-8) and "Let the Children Come: The Value of Children" (pp. 9-10).

How Young Children Learn

By Wes Haystead

How do you learn? How do you acquire information or develop opinions? Perhaps you do this by reading a book, by listening to a lecture or by talking with someone else. Much adult learning is by means of words—the symbols by which we are able to communicate.

However, learning in early childhood is different from learning as an adult. The mind of the child is not yet capable of handling ideas expressed only in words. The young child does not have the ability to give real meaning to a word unless the word is a very familiar part of experience and evokes ideas and feelings from memory.

Through the Senses

While we cannot know all that occurs in the mind of a young child, we do know that information enters the mind through the gates of the senses—seeing, touching, smelling, tasting and hearing.

Firsthand experiences are the hard core of learning for young children. Efforts to produce learning must involve as many of the

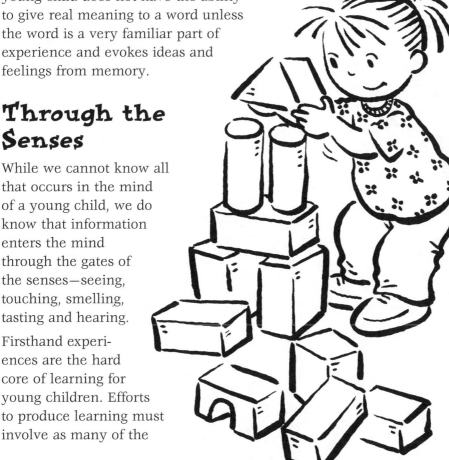

child's five senses as possible. Watching videos, sitting in large groups to sing songs and drawing on coloring pages are activities of limited value, as they involve only portions of the child's senses. Quality Christian education requires much more. Building with blocks, exploring natural items and participating in art and dramatic play are activities of great value, as they often engage the total child.

By Repetition

Repetition is a necessary and natural part of a young child's learning. A child who feels happy and satisfied with a learning experience will want to repeat it. Songs and stories become favorites only when they are enjoyed over and over.

By Practice in Play

The child also needs opportunities to practice behaviors that reflect Christian values. Repetition through play strengthens habits, attitudes, knowledge and understanding. Children learn because they are doing. And for young children, doing is play.

Play does not sound very educational or spiritual. But play is a child's full-time occupation: It is the activity through which the child learns best. Adults often distinguish between work and play. Not so with young children! Blocks, crayons, dolls, play dough and toy cars are the tools children use in play. They are tools by which children can also learn Bible truth when guided by alert teachers.

By Imitation

From infancy the child continually picks up ways of doing things from observation of others. A teacher's role, therefore, is not just to do "teacher things" but also to participate with children in the midst of their

activity. If you show kindness by sharing a crayon or marker, children will learn to share. If you thank God for making the colors in a fabric collage children are gluing, they will learn to pray in the midst of daily activities.

By Connecting Words to Actions

Children have limited vocabularies and experience. This combination results in a limited ability to understand and combine concepts. When you and a child are building a house with blocks, you may think, *I'm glad I have a house to live in. God shows His love for me by providing a house!* The young child, however, may only think, *I like the way this house looks!* You must provide words that help the child respond to the activity and relate God to the event. Once this relationship is made, the child is able to think about God the next time he or she builds a house. Without your words, the activity would be simply another of many fun play experiences.

Most efforts to teach young children focus on the things adults want children to know. While accurate information is important and is expressed through words, words and facts are very imperfect vehicles for the learning child. In order to see long-term results for your efforts, all dimensions of a child's learning must be involved. Your role is not merely to transmit truth; you must also demonstrate truth in practical everyday activities.

Let the Little Children Come: The Value of Children

By Wes Haystead

Jesus said, "Let the little children come to me, and do not hinder them, for the kingdom of heaven belongs to such as these."
Matthew 19:14

The most striking thing about Jesus' encounter with these little ones is not that He interrupted an adult meeting to take time for some children. Nor is it surprising that He physically picked up the children and loved them. The remarkable part of this incident is Jesus' words. Most adults would have said something like "Let the little children come to me, and don't prevent them, for some day they will grow up and become important."

Jesus saw something in childhood besides the future. He recognized worth and value in the state of being a child, for He told the waiting adults in the crowd that children are important for what they are right now—"For the kingdom of heaven belongs to such as these."

We adults always seem to be looking to the future. This push for preparation robs childhood of much of its essence, as parents and teachers urge little ones hurriedly through the present in search of a more significant future.

The Future—Now

"I know it's hard for a three-year-old to sit quietly and listen, but I have to start getting him ready for later when he will have to sit still."

"If he's going to be a success in life, he'll have to go to college. And to make sure he can stay ahead in school, I'm going to teach him to read before he starts first grade if it kills us both!"

"If a child is going to grow up with an appreciation for the great hymns of the church, you just can't start too young to teach them."

These and many similar statements are used repeatedly by parents and teachers who are earnestly concerned about helping young children get ready for future roles and demands. However, these well-meaning adults sometimes actually do more harm than good, because in their long-range view of growth they have lost sight of the value in just being a child.

Children are more than people in transition, waiting for some future date of real meaning.

The qualities that come from being young are not flaws or imperfections; rather, childhood is a marked and definable stage of development.

You may think, *But an adult has so many capabilities and accomplishments far beyond those of a child. Surely the years of productive and responsible adulthood are more significant than those of infancy and early childhood.* But what adult experiences could replace the laughter of children that gladdens the hearts of all who hear? How many hours of labor would it take to equal a little girl's smile? What a sterile world this would be were children not present to add their unique joys and sorrows!

The Value of a Child

Has any parent ever seen more deeply into him- or herself than when holding a newborn child and looking into that child's eyes? All the writings and research of humankind couldn't provide the insights that come with observing the experiences of a child starting out on his or her own unique adventure. The child's fresh enthusiasm for everything seen, the child's honest questions and powerfully simple logic—all combine to peel the scales from our encrusted adult eyes.

What is the value of a child—as a child? Incalculable!

This is no plea for attempting to stop the progress of maturation. This is simply a call to recognize that just because a phase of life is brief and is replaced by another more sophisticated, we should not rush past it; for if we bypass the unique stages of childhood, we strip each succeeding developmental stage of some of its finest ingredients. The best preparation for any phase of life is the proper completion of the previous one. The second coat of paint must always wait for the first to dry. Harvest never begins when the first green shoots appear in the spring. Human life has an aching void when childhood is squeezed away.

Is this what Jesus had in mind when He took a small child in His arms and said, "I tell you the truth, unless you change and become like little children, you will never enter the kingdom of heaven" (Matthew 18:3)? Is there a place in our homes and churches for children to be children? Do we wholeheartedly accept them as they are, not as we wish they were? Do the rooms and materials we provide sound out "Welcome!" to a young learner? Are the adults who surround young children deeply sympathetic and understanding of what these special years are all about?

Or do we merely see little ones in terms of their potential, enduring them until they get old enough to really matter? Is the church's objective in providing children's ministries a means of attracting their parents or of getting ready for the church of tomorrow? Is our goal to train young children to act like miniature adults because their noisy spontaneity might somehow mar our sacred corridors?

W.C. Fields wrung many laughs from his famous line, "Anyone who hates dogs and kids can't be all bad." But have you ever met a person who wanted to live in a world where everyone shared Fields's dislike of children?

It's far better to follow the Lord Jesus' pattern with children. His loving response to children lets us see into His heart's feeling of the worth of a young life.

Childhood is not a disease to be cured or endured. It is a God-ordained part of human life and has value and significance that continually enriches the experiences of those who may have forgotten what it is like to see the world from a fresh, unspoiled point of view.

Organizing Your Early Childhood Ministry

This section contains concise and practical information that can help you build a quality early childhood ministry from the ground floor up. There are two ways to find specific information you need:

1. Use the index at the back of this book to find specific information you need.
2. Read the section containing information on the subject you need help with.

Procedures are suggested for the following categories:

Programs and Curriculum: Gives an overview of the kinds of early childhood programs your church may choose to provide and gives tips on choosing which programs will most benefit your church and community. Includes guidelines for choosing curriculum and how to group children within various programs.

Staff: Describes everything you need to know about staffing your early childhood programs. Includes recruiting tips, job descriptions, screening and application forms, scheduling and training ideas, as well as tips for handling some frequent staff problems.

Facilities and Supplies: Provides complete descriptions of the well-equipped early childhood environment. Includes basic supply, equipment and furniture lists; room diagrams and tips for handling specific room problems.

Health and Safety: Describes vital information for making your early childhood classrooms safe for children. Includes suggestions and tips for keeping rooms clean, safety guidelines, check-in forms and ways to respond to illnesses and emergencies and more.

Parents and Family: Gives guidelines for communicating with parents and making it easy for parents to communicate with you. Describes parent handbooks and brochures, record keeping forms, plus ideas for family support and outreach.

Programs and Curriculum

Choosing Which Programs to Offer

Now more than ever, young children (and their parents) are encouraged to participate in a multitude of activities. As you survey the programs offered by churches and other organizations in your community, you will likely find an abundance of classes, field trips and other activities! How can a church decide what to offer? How can you know which programs will best meet the needs of the families in your church and community? In your role as a paid or volunteer director of early childhood ministry, you may have been asked to coordinate specific programs; or you may have the option to develop programs as you and others determine the needs of your church. For either situation, certain guidelines should be followed as you minister to the young children in your church.

Guideline One: Make a mental or written list of the different kinds of programs churches typically offer for young children and their families. Include programs such as Sunday School (on Sunday mornings or Saturday evenings or even during the week), second-hour programs, weekday programs, day care and special events (Mothers' Morning Out, Vacation Bible School, parenting classes, etc.). In addition, you may wish to consider special-interest programs such as art, drama or soccer classes. (Note: While many churches offer a weekday preschool or day care as part of their overall early childhood min-istry, this book is not intended to provide complete resources for organizing and administering a preschool or day-care program.)

Guideline Two: After listing the wide variety of potential program categories, narrow your focus. For each program you already have in place, write a brief one- or two-sentence description that answers the question, How does this program benefit young children and/or their families? For example, if you provide Sunday School classes, you might write "Sunday School classes benefit young children by teaching Bible stories and verses and introducing children to basic truths about God, Jesus, the Bible, prayer and the Church."

Guideline Three: Evaluate your overall ministry by considering such questions as:

• When do children and their families have opportunity to build relationships with each other?

• What programs help build bridges to children and families in our community?

• How do parents develop biblical parenting skills?

• What programs could meet the special needs of single parents or working parents?

• How do the programs for young children help fulfill the purpose or vision statement of our church?

In order to answer these questions and evaluate the early childhood ministry of your church, it's helpful to get the input of other people in the church. Ask parents of young children to complete the questionnaire on page 15. In addition, you may want to invite parents, past leaders, other staff, teachers and leaders in existing programs to a one-time meeting at which you brainstorm together possibilities for your early childhood ministry. Pray together, and ask God's wisdom and direction.

 **Guideline Four: Determine what your short-term (one to two years) and long-term (three to five years) goals are for ministry to young children and their families.** Consider what you can realistically provide based on the resources and size of your church. Don't be afraid to dream a little and explore new ministry ideas. To begin a new program, it's often easier to start with a short-term trial (for example, a mid-week program that meets once a week for six weeks rather than the entire year). And if you implement a program for six weeks and then discover it didn't work as well as planned, you are not committed for an entire year! Realize, also, that even if a program has been in place for many years, it's OK and probably beneficial to consider updating or reworking it (or even discarding it).

Choosing Curriculum

Once you have determined the programs your church will provide, begin looking for curriculum resources for each program. Request catalogs from church suppliers or browse among the resources at your local Christian bookstore or at the exhibits at a training conference. You may also ask for recommendations from early childhood directors at other churches. While it's often tempting to create your own material, it's easier to recruit staff if you can assure them of appropriate and complete resources. It is less time-consuming for teachers and leaders to adapt material to the specific needs of the children in their classes than to develop and write material entirely on their own.

If you are choosing curriculum for several different programs, as much as possible look for material that is consistent in philosophy and doctrine. While there may be more than one valid approach to learning, it is far more effective to train teachers to do one way well rather than to expect them to become skilled with varied materials that may be built on differing, even conflicting, educational and biblical principles.

For programs that are intended to provide regular Bible teaching such as Sunday School, use the curriculum guide on page 16. For other programs, adapt the curriculum guide to create a personalized checklist.

Parent Questionnaire

1. What programs at our church have your children participated in during the last six months?

2. Which of these programs would you like your children to attend again? What did you like about them?

3. How could these programs be improved?

4. In what specific ways have our church ministries helped improve your child's life? Your family life?

5. In what ways would you like further help for your child and/or family?

Compare Your Curriculum Options

Curriculum _____ Age Level _____

Use the following rating scale and questions to rate your curriculum options:

5 = Superior   4 = Excellent   3 = Good   2 = Fair   1 = Poor

Bible Content and Usage

____ Is the curriculum designed to teach the Bible as God's inspired and authoritative Word?

____ Is there balanced coverage of the Old and New Testaments?

____ Does the overall plan of the curriculum point students to faith in Christ as Savior and Lord, and also nurture and guide them to "grow up in Christ"?

____ Does the material present Bible truths in a manner appropriate to the abilities and development of the students' age levels?

____ Are hands-on Bible usage and skill development encouraged at appropriate age levels?

Teacher

____ Does the curriculum challenge the teacher to prepare spiritually for the task of teaching?

____ Is the material clearly arranged to show the teacher an understandable and logical lesson plan?

____ Are the Bible-learning and life-response aims specifically and clearly stated for each lesson?

____ Does the material provide the teacher with a variety of Bible learning activities?

____ Are the materials clearly presented, enabling the teacher to be prepared with a reasonable amount of effort?

____ Are there enough ideas and suggestions to adapt the material for longer or shorter sessions, larger or smaller groups, or limited equipment?

____ Does the curriculum give teaching tips to improve teachers's skills?

Student

____ Is the vocabulary appropriate for the age and abilities of the students?

____ Does the curriculum provide a variety of ways for students to participate actively in the learning process?

____ Are the student materials attractive and do they encourage involvement?

____ Do the teacher resources provide a variety of attractive aids to stimulate student interest and involvement?

____ Are the Bible-learning activities appropriate to the mental, spiritual, social and physical development of the students?

Beyond the Classroom

____ Does the material provide ideas for making and sustaining meaningful contact with both students and families outside the classroom?

____ Does the take-home paper contain activities that assist the family in relating the student's learning to everyday life?

____ Does the curriculum speak to issues relevant to the student's everyday life?

____ Does the curriculum provide materials and suggestions for ways students may understand the privilege and joy of sharing Christ?

____ Does the curriculum encourage outreach and church growth?

Grouping Children

Grouping young children is a significant part of planning and organizing your programs. Every church needs a well-thought-out policy about grouping and promoting young children. This policy needs to be clearly stated and communicated to parents and teachers. You can best group children by following certain guidelines.

 **Guideline One: All children and teachers benefit when classes are maintained at sizes similar to each other.**

Attendance records can help you do an effective job of determining class divisions. (See sample check-in form on p. 66.) The maximum number of children that should be in any early childhood classroom is shown in the chart below (for safety, two teachers should be present in each classroom):

An overcrowded group of three-year-olds next door to a nearly empty room of twos is not effective teaching. Each year evalu-ate the dividing line between the classes. Just because the current age-level divisions worked well last year does not mean they will be appropriate this year—unless, of course, your church can devise a system to get young couples to evenly space the arrival of new babies. (Note: During the summer months, if you regularly have fewer children attending than during the school year, you may wish to combine several ages in one class.)

During the school year, when a class has grown so large that it needs to be divided, create a smooth transition in the following manner:

• Have the new teachers sit in the class with the current teachers to observe and become better acquainted with the children.

• For several weeks, ask the new teachers to assume some of the teaching responsibilities.

• After several weeks, when teachers and children are well acquainted, create two classes with two or more teachers leading each class.

Grouping Children

Ages of children	Teacher to child ratio*	Maximum number of children per room
2-year-olds	1 to 3 or 4	12 to 15
2- and 3-year-olds	1 to 5	16 to 20
4- and 5-year-olds	1 to 6	20 to 24
Kindergarten	1 to 6	20 to 24

*See page 21 for more information on teacher/child ratios.

 **Guideline Two: Age is the safest criterion to use in dividing classes, and it is not necessary that the same date be used in dividing all classes.** In order to maintain balanced class sizes, it is perfectly reasonable to have one class include a 13-month span while the class next door has only an 11-month span. To avoid confusion, clearly post on the door of each class the specific age range of that group.

ROOM 6

Three-Year-Olds

For Children Whose Third Birthday Was Between December 15 and August 31

Teachers: Jean Smith and Sally Wong

 **Guideline Three: Children benefit more by being in a smaller group with more personal attention than by being in a large overcrowded group.** In the example on the previous page, everyone would benefit from placing the younger threes back with the two-year-olds where they could receive more individual care and guidance.

 **Guideline Four: The oldest early childhood class needs to align its policy with the local schools so that children are promoted into the elementary division when the child is ready to begin first grade.** If a parent decides to hold a younger child out of kindergarten for a year, it is best that the child remain in the early childhood class at church until he or she actually enters first grade. Teachers who have older children in their class need to be alert for enrichment ideas to keep these children from getting bored with activities designed for younger children. Your curriculum may provide kindergarten challenge ideas, but if not, teachers can add materials to Bible learning activities (greater variety of blocks, interesting art materials, etc.) or plan ways for children to use their increasing interests and abilities in reading and writing (dictate comments or stories, look at the words of a Bible verse in your Bible, etc.).

 **Guideline Five: Plan ahead to make promotion of children from one class to the next a positive experience.** Children move from one class to the next as a group at the start of the school year (or another time of year designated by your church policy). Designate a specific Sunday as Promotion Sunday or Graduation Sunday, coordinating this day with the elementary-age classes.

On Promotion Sunday (or any Sunday on which children change classes from one age level to the next, or when a new team of teachers begin teaching) children begin classes with their current teachers and at an announced time are escorted to their new classes for a get-acquainted time with their new teachers. Another option is for children to simply attend their new classes on Promotion Sunday. Whichever option you choose, be sure ahead of time to send parents information specifying the date of Promotion Sunday and the teachers' names and locations of all classes. In a large church, it will be helpful to have additional greeters available to help parents find their child's new classroom and to display class lists with maps in a variety of visible places in high traffic areas. (Don't forget to give ushers, greeters at welcome booths, etc., the appropriate information for guiding visitors to the correct places.)

Some parents may request that their children be moved ahead to an older class before Promotion Sunday. While occasionally a very small church may be able to accommodate such parent requests, it is usually best to keep children in their appropriate age-level class (the same age group with whom the child will later attend school) to avoid overcrowdiing caused by unplanned promotions. Discuss with the parents and teachers how the child's needs and interests can be met in the classroom.

Guideline Six: At least one class (or department in a church with more than one class for each age level) needs to be designated as a "holding class." In a holding class, children are received from a younger group more than once a year (for example, near the time of their birthdays) but are promoted out to the next older group all at one time. As a general rule of thumb, the class of two-year-olds (or the class of three-year-olds if two-year-olds are kept in the nursery) works best as the holding class. The holding class requires a very adaptable staff, since this class may be very small at the start of the year but may grow continually as children continue to be promoted into the class throughout the year.

It is best not to promote children into the holding class one at a time on their birthdays but to have periodic promotion days when all those who have reached a designated age or developmental milestone (walking, potty-trained, etc.) are moved to the next class as a group. Teachers in both classes can then prepare themselves, the parents and the children to make the promotion a positive experience. Children find it easier to make the change if accompanied by at least one friend.

Questions and Answers

My church is too small to have separate age-level classes. We combine all our preschoolers into one class. What should we know about how to combine mixed ages effectively?

Many small churches find it necessary to combine ages. Large churches may find it necessary to combine ages if their classroom space is limited or if unexpected growth takes place. Mixed-age classes provide benefits in younger children learning from older ones and older ones gaining from the opportunity to show responsibility.

First, consider the safety of the children in the mixed-age class. Evaluate the equipment and materials used to make sure they are safe for the youngest children who will be in the class. If materials are used which are not safe for the youngest children, they should be brought into the classroom for a specific activity and then used only under close supervision.

Second, provide curriculum for the age level of which you have the most children. Teachers can then adapt the activities for younger and/or older children.

Third, with classes of mixed ages, it is vital to provide the recommended number of teachers so that the youngest children are cared for adequately and the oldest children are challenged appropriately. An understaffed group of mixed ages is likely to provide a significant amount of negative rather than positive learning.

  Some churches include kindergarten children with elementary age children. Is this a good idea?

Early childhood classes have traditionally included all children who have not yet started first grade. However, many educators, parents and church leaders now feel that kindergarten children fit better with younger elementary children than with older preschoolers.

The main reason for this view is that most children by this age have already had extensive classroom experience in day care and/or preschool before beginning kindergarten. No longer is this the age when most young children encounter their first group learning situation, and many kindergarten children already possess some of the cognitive skills (beginning reading, writing, math, etc.) previously introduced in first grade.

However, there are valid reasons to be cautious about attempting to merge kindergartners with elementary-aged children. Kindergartners still need the informal, physically active session plan that is the hallmark of early childhood. And children of this age still learn most effectively through hands-on experiences coupled with a teacher's guided conversation. Attempts to accelerate them into groups, activities, materials and schedules designed for older children might harm the children's development. In most cases, the emotional, social, physical and mental needs of kindergartners are better met by providing them with one more year of early childhood, guided by teachers who are aware of the great learning strides being made in this exciting year of life.

  We provide programs for children for more than one hour on a Sunday morning. What are the special needs of children that we should consider?

As you develop the schedule for the total morning, realize that the children in your care will not be able to sit still for long periods of time. The youngest will likely not be able to sit still for any period of time! Be sure to alternate quiet activities with activities that allow children to exercise their large-muscles (active games, blocks, playground play, etc.). If children attend a portion of the adult worship service before a session begins, provide a large-motor activity at the beginning of the session.

Read "Schedule: Guidelines for Making Your Class Schedule Work" on pages 153-156 for a recommended Sunday School session schedule. Sessions that take place either before or after Sunday School typically provide a combination of activity centers, Bible story and worship times, snack and/or supervised outdoor or indoor play. It is best if all sessions in which young children are involved focus on one Bible story and verse in a single morning. Then children are provided with the repetition so necessary for early childhood learners and are less likely to become confused by information from one or more Bible stories.

Staff

Teacher/Child Ratios

Special consideration needs to be given in planning the number of staff needed for early childhood programs. Safety issues are often a big concern to parents; they will be reassured if they see adequate adult supervision. More than physical safety, however, parents want to know that their child will be cared for and loved as an individual, not as simply one of many in a crowded room. A small teacher/child ratio also helps more effective learning take place because teachers can give attention to each child. In order to meet these needs, specific teacher/child ratios are recommended for programs involving young children.

Teacher/Child Ratios

Ages of children	Teacher to child ratio	Maximum number of children per room*
2-year-olds	1 to 3 or 4	12 to 15
2- and 3-year-olds	1 to 5	16 to 20
4- and 5-year-olds	1 to 6	20 to 24
Kindergarten	1 to 6	20 to 24

*See page 17 for more information on grouping young children.

The benefits of maintaining appropriate teacher/child ratios are many—the teacher is more apt to build relationships with individual children, follow up on absentees and visitors, extend outreach to families of class members and remember special occasions such as birthdays. Teachers with too many children in their classes often don't attempt follow-up and outreach because the tasks appear overwhelming, and these teachers may also feel that there are already more children than they can teach (or have room for) in their classes.

As a rule of thumb, every classroom should always have a minimum of two adults in case of emergency. (See pp. 76-77 for additional safety precautions of which your church should be aware in order to prevent legal liability.)

Some people question these ratios when some weekday preschools and kindergartens consistently operate with 8 to 30 children per teacher. There are some significant reasons why the larger ratios are not appropriate for a church's once-a-week programs:

• Large teacher/child ratios in weekday programs are imposed for economic, not educational, reasons. The people most closely involved in these programs clearly recognize that children in large groups do not receive the quality care or instruction they really need and deserve. A large percentage of these programs utilize part-time or volunteer aides to reduce the ratios and provide the personal touch each child needs.

• Most once-a-week church ministries are staffed and supervised by volunteers who often have very minimal time for training and preparation. Expecting these volunteers to work with the same group sizes as professionals is a good way to discourage volunteers.

• Weekday programs have the children for 2½ hours or more per day, two to five days per week. The teacher is able to ensure that each child gets some personal attention at some time during every week. The one-day-a-week programs of the church do not allow the teacher time to have significant personal interaction with every child if the suggested ratios are exceeded.

• Relationships between teachers and children are the most powerful dimension of the church's ministry. While it may be possible to entertain with videos a large group of young children or to supervise a large group who are all involved in one activity, the church has a higher calling: to love children in a personal, individual way that gives each child a glimpse of God's everlasting love for them.

Job Descriptions

Your teachers and helpers will find their jobs easier if their assigned tasks are clear and specific. Write (and update periodically as needed) a job description for each position in your early childhood ministry. Distribute the job descriptions to the appropriate staff, and use the descriptions as an aid to recruiting. If you have a rotating staff, also display the job descriptions in the early childhood rooms at the appropriate locations.

Depending on the size of your church, your early childhood staff may include a variety of jobs: Sunday School coordinator, lead teacher, teacher, helper, greeter, food coordinator, substitute and supply coordinator.

All job descriptions should include starting and ending dates (preferably six months to a year; read more about that on p. 26), general description of the job (one to three sentences), name and phone number of supervisor, specific tasks (include times, locations, etc.) and what support will be provided (curriculum and materials provided, training opportunities, etc.). Job descriptions may also include expected times of arrival and departure, how to maintain cleanliness in the room during and after the session, suggested schedules and what to do in case of emergencies or problems.

Adapt the following job descriptions, adding information specific to your church and adding appropriate information if any positions are filled by paid workers.

Sunday School Coordinator

Task: To plan and develop a program of Bible learning through loving adult care, Bible stories and Bible learning activities for preschool children each Sunday morning

Term: One year, beginning September 1

Supervisor and Phone Number:

_____

Individual Responsibilities:

• Maintain a personal relationship with Jesus Christ.

• Desire to grow in faith and commitment to God and participate in personal Bible study and prayer.

• Worship regularly with the church family.

Team Responsibilities:

• Recruit leaders, teachers and helpers for all Sunday School classes.

• Plan and lead a regular program of training for all Sunday School staff.

• Observe, evaluate and affirm teachers in order to note strengths to encourage and areas where improvement is possible.

• Pray regularly for Sunday School leaders, teachers and helpers.

• Lead regular planning meetings for teachers and helpers that include training and opportunities for spiritual growth.

• Oversee the purchase, distribution and use of all equipment and supplies (curriculum, snacks, art supplies, etc.).

• Communicate the church's approved safety policy to all Sunday School staff, regularly evaluate its use, and take necessary steps to put the policy into practice.

• Plan Sunday School staff fellowship/training events at least twice a year in order to encourage excellence in teaching skills and to build a sense of teamwork among all teachers.

• Express appreciation to the Sunday School staff, including an end-of-the-year event.

• Communicate with parents regarding the purpose, value and procedures of Sunday School.

• Communicate regularly with supervisor and teachers of related programs (weekday preschool, second-hour coordinator, etc.).

Note: Depending on the size of your church, the Sunday School coordinator may have responsibility for the entire Sunday School or just one age level.

Lead Teacher

Tasks: To prayerfully build relationships with both teachers and children, to ensure effective Bible learning and to participate in classroom activities

Term: One year, beginning September 1

Supervisor and Phone Number:

_____

Individual Responsibilities:

• Maintain a personal relationship with Jesus Christ.

• Desire to grow in faith and commitment to God and participate in personal Bible study and prayer.

• Worship regularly with the church family.

Team Responsibilities:

• Coordinate teacher tasks, including use of supplies and room setup.

• Pray regularly for others on the teaching team.

• Work with your supervisor to identify and enlist qualified people to join your teaching team.

• Lead regular session planning meetings, including training and opportunities for spiritual growth.

• Plan a team get-together in order to build friendships among the team once a quarter.

• Communicate regularly with supervisor.

Sunday Morning Responsibilities:

• Greet children as they arrive and guide them to an activity.

• Assist teachers as needed (discipline, activity completion, etc.), maintaining the time schedule for the session.

• Observe, evaluate and affirm teachers, noting strengths to be encouraged and areas to be improved.

• Lead the large-group learning time, involving other teachers as appropriate.

Note: In a class with just two teachers, the lead teacher responsibilities may be informally shared. When three or more people are on the team, one person should be designated as the lead teacher.

Teacher

Task: To prayerfully build relationships with children in order to guide them in life-changing Bible learning

Term: One year, beginning September 1

Supervisor and Phone Number:

_____

Individual Responsibilities:

• Maintain a personal relationship with Jesus Christ.

• Desire to grow in faith and commitment to God and participate in personal Bible study and prayer.

• Worship regularly with the church family.

Team Responsibilities:

• Pray regularly for each child and others on your teaching team.

• Participate in scheduled teachers' meetings.

• Participate in at least one training event during the year to improve teaching skills.

• Express needs as a teacher to lead teacher or Sunday School coordinator.

Sunday Morning Responsibilities:

• Arrange materials and room to create an effective learning environment.

• Greet each child upon arrival and involve him or her in conversation and meaningful activity.

• Model the love of Christ by getting to know children and sharing their concerns, needs and joys.

• Guide Bible learning by:
1. being well prepared to use Bible stories, Bible verses, questions and comments appropriate to the age level in order to accomplish the lesson aims;
2. selecting a variety of Bible learning activities and encouraging each child to actively participate in each lesson;
3. participating with children in learning activities and in large-group times.

Student Follow-Up Responsibilities:

• Follow up on visitors and absentees with mailings, phone calls and/or personal visits.

• Care for each class member with prayer, telephone calls, birthday cards, etc.

• Communicate individual children's needs to parents.

Helper

Task: To prayerfully build relationships with children in order to guide them in life-changing Bible learning

Term: One year, beginning September 1

Supervisor and Phone Number:

_____

Individual Responsibilities:

• Maintain a personal relationship with Jesus Christ.

• Desire to grow in faith and commitment to God and participate in personal Bible study and prayer.

• Worship regularly with the church family.

Team Responsibilities:

• Pray regularly for each child and others on your teaching team.

• Participate in scheduled teachers' meetings.

Sunday Morning Responsibilities:

• Greet each child upon arrival and involve him or her in conversation and meaningful activity.

• Model the love of Christ by getting to know children and sharing their concerns, needs and joys.

• Guide Bible learning by:
  1. assist teacher in using Bible stories, Bible verses, questions and comments appropriate to the age level in order to accomplish the lesson aims;
  2. encouraging each child to actively participate in each lesson;
  3. participating with children in learning activities and in large-group times.

Greeter

Tasks: To greet families and check in children as they arrive for Sunday School.

Term: Six months, September through February or March through August

Supervisor and Phone Number:

_____

Individual Responsibilities:

• Maintain a personal relationship with Jesus Christ.

• Desire to grow in faith and commitment to God and participate in personal Bible study and prayer.

• Worship regularly with the church family.

Sunday Morning Responsibilities:

• Be present in the classroom from 9:30 A.M. until 10:00 A.M. each Sunday morning.

• Put out a new check-in form each Sunday. Place previous check-in form in the attendance-form box in the reception office.

• Assist parent(s) as needed to check in.

• Offer a friendly greeting to each family, alerting families to any special announcements or procedural changes.

• Pay special attention to visitors. Get names and addresses, give name tags, direct children and parents to appropriate rooms, etc.

• Communicate regularly with supervisor.

Food Coordinator

Task: To oversee the provision of food (snacks, meals, etc.) when needed at Sunday School and other early childhood programs

Term: One year, beginning September 1

Supervisor and Phone Number:

_____

Individual Responsibilities:

• Maintain a personal relationship with Jesus Christ.

• Desire to grow in faith and commitment to God and participate in personal Bible study and prayer.

• Worship regularly with the church family.

Team Responsibilities:

• Determine the food needs for all early childhood programs, working with early childhood ministry leaders.

• Provide food through purchases and donations of money or food. If parents are asked to provide food, set up and oversee a schedule of donations.

Supply Coordinator

Task: To purchase distribute and organize teaching supplies

Term: One year, beginning September 1

Supervisor and Phone Number:

_____

Individual Responsibilities:

• Maintain a personal relationship with Jesus Christ.

• Desire to grow in faith and commitment to God and participate in personal Bible study and prayer.

• Worship regularly with the church family.

Team Responsibilities:

• Inventory and purchase needed supplies (obtain approval from Sunday School Coordinator for purchases over $25.00).

• Turn in receipts to church office for reimbursement.

• Keep records of all purchases.

• Organize and maintain supply room

• Help determine Sunday School budget.

Substitute

Task: To serve as substitute for teacher(s) as needed

Term: One year, beginning September 1

Supervisor and Phone Number:

_____

Individual Responsibilities:

• Maintain a personal relationship with Jesus Christ.

• Desire to grow in faith and commitment to God and participate in personal Bible study and prayer.

• Worship regularly with the church family.

Team Responsibilities:

• Pray regularly for teachers for whom you will substitute.

• Participate in at least one training event during the year to improve teaching skills.

Sunday Morning Responsibilities:

• Greet each child upon arrival and involve him or her in conversation and meaningful activity.

• Model the love of Christ by getting to know children and sharing their concerns, needs and joys.

• Guide Bible learning by:
1. following instructions in curriculum for using Bible stories, Bible verses, questions and comments appropriate to the age level in order to accomplish the lesson aims;
2. encouraging each child to actively participate in each lesson;
3. participating with children in learning activities and in large-group times.

Term of Service

As life gets busier and busier with seemingly fewer hours in every day, churches continually struggle with recruiting teachers who will serve on a continuing and regular basis. While people serving in support tasks (record keeping, supplies, etc.) may be willing to commit to a year of service, you may experience difficulty in obtaining year-long commitments from people serving as teachers.

Continuity of care is an ideal to strive for constantly. Young children benefit significantly from the security of familiar people in charge of the program. This security creates fewer discipline problems, and more positive learning can take place.

Children aren't the only ones who benefit from consistent teachers. Adults who spend their time teaching children will also find their experience much more enjoyable (and hopefully serve more often) if they are given the opportunity to get to know the children in their classes, learning about each one and appreciating their growth and development.

The ideal plan is to schedule teachers for 12 months at a time. Some churches recruit teachers for the school year, with a different staff for the summer months. Helpers or aides may be asked to commit for terms of one or more consecutive months. (If helpers serve for one month at a time, schedule their terms of service so that they overlap, resulting in some new and some familiar faces each week.)

A system of one-Sunday-a-month teachers or helpers has not proven satisfactory in meeting children's educational and emotional needs, and occasional volunteers never develop a sense of the value of this ministry. The overwhelming attitude in such situations is "I'll take my turn, but don't expect me to like it or to become good at it." In this plan, the coordinator also becomes overwhelmed at the logistics of scheduling, training and distributing materials on a weekly basis.

Recruiting Guidelines

Keeping a positive attitude about recruiting can be a challenge. A lack of congregational awareness of the early childhood ministry, and adults who feel that they are too busy or that they've done their time in teaching children are barriers many churches face.

 **Guideline One: Plan ongoing publicity.** Begin by developing an ongoing plan to publicize the positive benefits of your early childhood ministry. On a regular basis, enthusiastically present to the congregation information about the goals, benefits and opportunities for ministry with children. (You may need to coordinate your efforts with the leaders of other age-level ministries.) People do not want to make a commitment to a program about which they are unfamiliar. Nor do they get excited about becoming part of a group which always seems to be making desperate appeals for help.

Consider scheduling one of these publicity ideas every month or two throughout the year:

• photos of children and teachers displayed in newsletters or bulletin boards (see sketch on next page)

• brief newsletter articles written by teachers or parents about their experience in an early childhood program

• interviews in adult classes of early childhood teachers

• displays of early childhood art in well-traveled areas of your facility

• quotes of interesting or humorous things children say in Sunday School

• brief statements about the value of Christian education coupled with an invitation to pray for the church's ministry to preschoolers

The major benefit of these publicity ideas comes when you use them in advance of and during times when you are actively recruiting people to serve.

 **Guideline Two: List potential staff.** Continually identify potential staff for your early childhood programs, keeping in mind the goal of helping people find fulfilling places of ministry. Avoid the trap of only looking for prospective staff when you face a vacancy. By actively seeking to discover people with the potential for ministry, the focus can be on finding the position which fits the person, rather than trying to squeeze the person into the job.

Consider everyone in your congregation in your recruiting efforts. Use the church membership list, new members' classes, adult class lists, suggestions from adult teachers or leaders, lists of previous teachers and survey forms. Consider parents, singles, seniors and collegians. Get recommendations from present teachers. Look for people whom you have observed interacting in positive ways with young children. (Limit your use of teens to times of ministry when their own groups are not meeting.)

Ask others to help you in your recruiting effort. The total church staff needs to accept part of the concern for recruitment. The pastor, Christian education board, Sunday School coordinators, teachers and helpers must support, encourage and, above all, pray that potential teachers will accept an invitation to ministry. If recruiting is the responsibility of only two or three people, those people often become overworked and discouraged—and recruitment prospects are limited to the friends and acquaintances of these few people.

This involvement does not mean everyone is trying to sign up new teachers. Rather, everyone on the staff must be informed of recruiting needs, pray regularly that the needs will be met and be willing to help where appropriate in the recruiting process. In a larger church, it is often helpful to have a committee that is responsible for the various steps in effective recruiting. Form a new committee at least once a year. Invite people to be on the committee who know a wide variety of people within the congregation and who have skills in a variety of areas: publicity, teacher appreciation, new teacher orientation, personal contact, etc.

Guideline Three: Contact potential staff.

After your list is made, prayerfully prioritize it. Of all the people who could possibly be contacted, who should be approached first? Determine any requirements a person must meet in order to be considered. Involve responsible leaders in your church in evaluating or approving those to be contacted. Your church may have established guidelines for volunteers (length of church attendance or membership, etc.). Some prospects may need to be eliminated from consideration because of other commitments they have made of which you are unaware.

Then personally contact each prospective teacher or helper by phone or by mail. People who are recruited in the halls or parking lot of a church may feel as though both they and the job are of less than crucial importance. If you choose to send a form letter to your prospects, add a personal note to the letter. Do not depend on recruiting announcements in church bulletins or newsletters; it's best to personally recruit from a pool of people who have been recommended to you or who have demonstrated the characteristics of the kind of teachers you're looking for.

Schedule a personal meeting or phone conversation that allows an unhurried period of time in which you and the prospect can get better acquainted, answer each other's questions and clarify information as needed. If the initial contact is by mail, follow up the letter with a phone call. Never underestimate the importance of personal contact or expect that people will join your staff simply because they received a letter in the mail. A job description should be made available to each prospect (see sample job descriptions on pp. 22-25).

When a large number of teaching positions are to be filled, consider setting up a display in a well-traveled area of your church. A large attractive poster will attract attention as will a video or photographs of the program for which you are recruiting. If you want to display a list of jobs to be filled, be sure to show that a significant number of positions are already filled. No one wants to be the first to sign up!

Many churches find it effective to develop a recruiting theme for each year's efforts. These themes (slogans and artwork) can be used in letters to preselected prospects, in bulletin or newsletter announcements and in recruiting displays (see sample logos on this page and p. 29).

When you talk with a prospective teacher or helper, answer questions, offer a time of observation in the appropriate early childhood program and encourage him or her to prayerfully consider this opportunity. Agree on a time by which the decision will be made, usually about a week. If the answer is yes, be ready to offer orientation and training to help the new staff member make a good beginning. If the answer is no, thank the prospect for taking the time to consider the ministry.

Screening Volunteers

An important step in the recruiting process is establishing a set of procedures to be followed in screening and approving volunteers. Determine with others in your church

Keep the Promise.
Be a Teacher!

Give Your Faith Away!

Teachers Unlock the Future

Teachers Have BIG Ideas

You Can Make a Difference!

Our Kids Are Counting on You

the procedures your church will follow to protect both children and volunteers. Consider consulting a legal expert in church liability issues who is familiar with the applicable laws in your state.

Application Forms: Every person who is a volunteer or paid member of your staff should be asked to fill out an application form (see sample on pp. 31-32). Carefully evaluate the information on the form and, if needed, contact the references listed. All applications and reference checks are required to be kept confidential.

Personal Interview: If you are in a large church where people are being contacted who are not well known to others, you may wish to set up an interviewing team of two people to meet with people who have agreed to accept a teaching position. In the interview, review the information on the application form. Talk informally about the person's background and interest in ministry. The purpose of the interview is to get acquainted with the potential teacher so that you are able to assess the person's skills and abilities in a more personal way than in a written statement.

Fingerprinting and Background Checks: Some churches require fingerprinting and police background checks for all staff who work with children. (Check with your local police department or state Department of Justice for information on how such checks are handled in your area.)

Safety Policy: Developing a safety policy for preventing and reporting child abuse and endangerment is an important step in the screening process. While a problem is never expected, it is wise to take necessary precautions by developing a written safety policy. All staff should read the safety policy and each year sign a form verifying their compliance with the policy. A safety policy should include:

• guidelines for teacher selection (including some or all of the following: application forms, personal interviews, follow-up of references, fingerprinting and criminal history checks);

• policies to be followed in the classroom and on any church-sponsored outings (number of adults required, name tags, check-in and check-out procedures, rest room guidelines, etc.);

• reporting obligations on the part of teachers if child abuse is observed or suspected;

• step-by-step plans for response to an allegation of child abuse.

Church leaders should approve the safety policy, and all staff should be familiarized with the policy on an annual basis. It is also recommended that a lawyer evaluate your policy to be sure it conforms to your state's laws regarding the reporting of child abuse. Depending on the kinds of ministry your church provides, you may need to check with your state's social services department to determine licensing laws that apply to church programs such as day care, summer sessions, etc.

It is always best to present the safety policy with an introduction explaining the purpose of such a policy: to make your church the best place it can be for the children in your community and to protect teachers should allegations of abuse or child endangerment be made. Use the sample Child Safety Policy and Introductory Letter on pages 33-35 as guides in developing your own procedures.

If someone unknown to you or other members of your church requests to teach or help with children in your ministry, sincerely thank the person for his or her offer. Explain that all staff are required to have regularly attended the church for a minimum of six months to a year (or whatever your church's policy specifies). Be ready to suggest a way the person might help in the program until the time requirement has been met (decorate bulletin boards, help with mailings, etc.) or another area of service in the church.

Volunteer Application Form

IMPORTANT: *This is a sample form, not intended to be reproduced. Adapt to your specific needs.*

First Church has a child/youth safety policy founded on respect and love for the children and youth of our church and community. This safety policy gives children, youth, parents and all Sunday School staff a sense of confidence and peace. We ask your cooperation in completing and returning this application.

Personal Information

Name _____

Address _____ Phone Number _____

Best time to call: Morning _____ Afternoon _____ Evening _____

Day and month of birth _____

Occupation _____

Where employed _____ Phone Number _____

Can you receive calls at work?   ❑ Yes   ❑ No

Do you have a current driver's license?   ❑ Yes   ❑ No   License number _____

Children   ❑ Yes   ❑ No   Name(s) and age(s) _____

_____

Spouse   ❑ Yes   ❑ No   Name _____

Are you currently a member of First Church?   ❑ Yes   ❑ No   If yes, how long? _____

Please list other churches and locations where you have regularly attended over the past five years. _____

Have you read and do you agree to follow our child/youth safety policy? _____

Are you currently under a charge or have you ever been convicted of or pled guilty to child abuse or a crime involving actual or attempted sexual misconduct or sexual molestation of a minor?   ❑ Yes   ❑ No   If yes, please explain _____

Are you currently under a charge or have you ever been convicted guilty of or pled guilty to possession/sale of controlled substances or of driving under the influence of alcohol?

❑ Yes   ❑ No   If yes, please explain _____

_____

Is there any other information that we should know? _____
_____

Church Activity

1. Please write a brief statement of how you became a Christian.

_____

2. In what activities/ministries of our church are you presently involved?

_____

3. Experience:

   a. What volunteer or career experiences with children/youth have you had in the church or the community? _____

   b. List any gifts, calling, training, education or other factors that have prepared you for ministry to children/youth _____

4. Preferences: In what capacity and with what age group would you like to minister?

_____

5. Concerns: What causes the greatest feelings of apprehension as you contemplate this ministry? _____

Personal References (Not a former employer or relative)

Name _____ Phone Number _____

Address _____

Name _____ Phone Number _____

Address _____

Applicant's Statement

The information contained in this application is true and correct to the best of my knowledge. I authorize any of the above references or churches to give you any information that they may have regarding my character and fitness to work with youth or children.

I hereby certify that I have read and that I understand the attached provisions of (insert title of your state's penal code regarding the reporting of child abuse and neglect).

Signature _____ Date _____

Child and Youth Safety Policy

IMPORTANT: *This is a sample form, not intended to be reproduced. Adapt to your specific needs.*

We desire to protect and support those who work with our youth and children. These policies to prevent child abuse, neglect or any unfounded allegations against workers or teachers address three major areas:

1. Worker selection
2. Worker practices
3. Reporting obligation

Selecting Youth and Children's Workers

• All paid employees, full or part-time, including clergy, and all volunteer children and youth workers should complete a Volunteer Application Form.

• A personal interview will be included as part of the selection process.

• Where circumstances merit, personal references listed in the application will be checked to further determine the suitability and character of the applicant. The reference check shall be documented.

• All workers with youth or children should normally be members of First Church or have been attending First Church for a minimum of six months.

Safety Policies for Youth Ministries

• Volunteers and other workers are encouraged to be in public areas where both the youth and teacher are visible to other people.

• All drivers transporting youth on out-of-town activities shall be a minimum age of 25 and maximum age of 65 and shall complete and have approved a Driver Form.

• The desirable minimum age for all drivers for in-town activities is 25. No one under age 18 will be permitted to drive for any church-sponsored activity.

• Youth workers should not provide transportation to and from church on a regular basis.

• For overnight outings and camps, whenever both genders are present as participants, both genders need to be present in leadership.

• For outdoor activities, participants are to be in groups of at least three.

• Counseling of youth is to be by a leader of the same gender and is to be done in public areas where both the youth and leader are visible to other people.

Safety Policies for Children's Ministries

• Each group of children should have at least two workers who are not related to each other, at least one being an adult, present at all times.

• For children, infant through kindergarten age, the desirable ratio is one worker for every five children. For grades one through five, the desirable ratio is one worker for each eight children.

• Window blinds and doors are to be kept open (or doors should have windows). A supervisor or designated adult representative will circulate where children's activities are occurring.

• When taking children to the rest room, workers should supervise children of the same gender. The worker should stay out of the rest room at the open door until the child is finished in the stall. Workers enter to assist only when necessary.

• All drivers transporting children on out-of-town activities shall be a minimum age of 25 and maximum age of 65 and shall complete and have approved a Driver Form.

• In the nursery, diapers are to be changed only in designated areas and in the presence of other caregivers.

Reporting Obligation and Procedure

1. All workers are to be familiar with the definitions of child abuse (see below).

2. If a worker suspects that a child has been abused, the following steps are to be followed:

   • Report the suspected abuse to your supervisor.
   • Do not interview the child regarding the suspected abuse. The interview process will be handled by trained personnel.
   • Do not discuss the suspected abuse. It is important that all information about the suspected child abuse (victim and abuser) be kept confidential.

3. Workers reporting suspected child abuse will be asked to complete the Suspected Child Abuse Report (available from your state's Department of Social Services). Confidentiality will be maintained where possible. This report must be completed within 24 hours.

4. Once a suspected child abuse case has been reported by a worker to a supervisor, it will be reported to the designated reporting agency.

Definitions of Child Abuse

Defined by The National Committee for Prevention of Child Abuse

Physical Abuse

Nonaccidental injury, which may include beatings, violent shaking, human bites, strangulation, suffocation, poisoning, or burns. The results may be bruises and welts, broken bones, scars, permanent disfigurement, long-lasting psychological damage, serious internal injuries, brain damage, or death.

Neglect

The failure to provide a child with basic needs, including food, clothing, education, shelter, and medical care; also abandonment and inadequate supervision.

Sexual Abuse

The sexual exploitation of a child by an older person, as in rape, incest, fondling of the genitals, exhibitionism, or pornography. It may be done for the sexual gratification of the older person, out of a need for power, or for economic reasons.

Safety Policy Introductory Letter

IMPORTANT: *This is a sample form, not intended to be reproduced. Adapt to your specific needs.*

(Date)

(Church Name)

(Address)

(Phone Number)

Dear _____ ,
                    (name)

Here at First Church we believe that having a well-thought-out Child and Youth Safety Policy is part of the wisdom to which Christ calls us. We are aware that even with such a policy in place, we remain dependent on Christ and His ultimate protection. However, this policy will give us confidence that our children and youth will have a safe environment in which to learn and grow in their Christian faith.

We are asking that everyone in the children's and youth ministries complete the required forms and attend a training session about the Child and Youth Safety Policy. The next training session is scheduled on (date). We thank you for your help and cooperation in advance.

Our efforts in this area are a bit like a CPR class. You never expect to have a problem, yet you take all the precautions you possibly can. You train in order to know how to respond if there is a situation calling for action, believing and praying that it will not be needed.

Thank you for caring about children and youth and helping them grow in the nurture and admonition of the Lord.

Sincerely,

_____

(name)

_____

Pastor

New Teacher Orientation

When a new volunteer makes a commitment to serve on your staff, the training phase of your recruitment program begins. You can't separate recruiting and training. Beginnings are the most important—and probably the most risky—times for a new recruit, so every possible help to assure his or her success is a must.

Meet with new teachers or helpers to explain the goals, methods, curriculum and organization of your Sunday School. Provide a copy of the current curriculum materials, policies and procedures that affect your staff; names and phone numbers of other teachers; a copy of the schedule of the class and a class roster. If you have more than one new staff member, communicate this information in an orientation class. Distribute a copy of "Teacher Preparation: Get Prepared to Teach" on pages 171-172 for teachers to read. Use the information in the article to discuss helpful information that every teacher needs to know.

Many churches have found it helpful to develop a teacher handbook that is updated and distributed to staff at the beginning of the teaching term and to new teachers as they join the staff during the term. Handbooks can be brief, providing the information mentioned in the previous paragraph, or they can be extensive, providing articles related to teaching philosophy and skills.

When meeting with new teachers, it is helpful to list the specific tasks expected. In this list, try to answer the question, What are the basic things a person should do in order to succeed in this ministry? Include statements explaining why each action is important and how it will benefit the teacher by helping him or her succeed. (For example, "It is important to get each session off to a good start by allowing time for friendly informal conversations as children arrive. In order to allow for this relaxed beginning, teachers need to be in their rooms, ready to welcome and guide children, at least 10 minutes before the announced starting time of the session.") Take advantage of the orientation resources that correlate with the curriculum you use (walk-through cassettes, explanatory videos, etc.).

Some churches find it helpful to use one or both of the commitment forms on pages 37 and 38 as part of a new teacher's orientation. Signing these forms highlights the importance of your ministry.

Sunday School Contract

I, _____, because I feel called by God, commit to the following guidelines as a Sunday School teacher for the period of _____ to _____. This commitment is reviewable and renewable.

As a Sunday School teacher, I will

◆ Serve on the teaching team for the _____ class/department.

As a Sunday School teacher, I am committed to

Our Lord

◆ I have a personal relationship with Jesus Christ which I desire to model for children.

◆ I enjoy studying God's Word regularly and desire to grow in my faith and commitment to Him (through personal study, adult classes or home Bible study groups).

Our Church

◆ I worship regularly with our church family.

◆ I support the doctrinal statement and leadership of our church.

My Students

◆ I enjoy children and desire for them to know of God's love and concern for their lives.

◆ I will take the necessary time to prepare my lessons during the week, incorporating my own God-given gifts into each lesson.

◆ I will care for my students individually (through prayer, telephone calls, birthday cards, etc.).

◆ I will be faithful in attendance, arriving at least 15 minutes before the session begins. If I must be absent, I will contact an approved substitute and alert the Sunday School Coordinator.

◆ I will follow up with mailing or visits to absentee class members.

◆ I will participate in at least one training event during the year to improve my teaching skills.

My Teaching Team

◆ I will communicate regularly with my team teachers.

◆ I will participate in scheduled teachers' meetings.

◆ I will care for and return all equipment and curriculum provided.

◆ I will express my needs as a teacher to the Christian Education Committee.

_____

Teacher

The Christian Education Commitment to Sunday School Teachers

Acting as representatives for the Christian Education Committee, we commit to the following responsibilities:

◆ Be available to provide loving support, encouragement and counsel.

◆ Provide regularly scheduled opportunities for teacher growth—fellowship, training and coordinated planning.

◆ Review, recommend and provide curriculum resources.

◆ Recruit teachers and other staff as needed.

◆ Provide suitable supplies, environment and equipment.

◆ Plan special events to stimulate interest in the Sunday School.

◆ Encourage communication between teachers, parents and church leaders.

_____

Christian Education Representative

_____

Sunday School Coordinator

If a new volunteer is joining a class already in progress, arrange for the new person to observe and assist an experienced teacher several times. If the teachers in the class are meeting to plan, invite the new volunteer to attend. Give the new volunteer a simple assignment or two as a starter for the next Sunday. Increase the areas of responsibility each week as the new worker shows ability and confidence.

Consider planning a basic orientation course that presents key topics: how young children learn, age characteristics and needs of children, discipline tips, storytelling guidelines, etc. Larger churches may have enough new teachers that they conduct orientation courses as part of their adult education program. (Orientation courses can be coordinated with leaders of other age levels.) Some churches have even found that inviting the entire congregation to attend training events helps participants determine if they are gifted in the area of teaching.

Training

Effective teacher training is an essential ingredient in any church that seeks to build a quality ministry to young children. Each session in any program brings new children and/or new challenges, requiring teachers who are growing in their ministry. All staff members need repeated exposure to essential goals and procedures in order to keep their enthusiasm high and for consistency in the overall program. Even experienced teachers need opportunities to be refreshed and to evaluate their efforts.

The focus of training should always be on specific skills the teachers can implement in their next class session. In addition, teachers should be shown how their curriculum resources can be used most effectively. Plan a year-long training schedule making use of one or more of the training methods suggested below. Adapt the sample plan on the next page according to the needs of your church.

A Sample One-Year Training/Communicating Plan

Month	Topic	Page Numbers Articles for Use in Meeting or Newsletter	Mini-poster
September	Characteristics	97	197
October	Teacher's Role	173	195
November	Schedule	153	191
December	Discipline	109	181
January	How Young Children Learn	7	207
February	Storytelling	165	205
March	Learning Styles	131	185
April	Guided Conversation	127	183
May	Salvation	151	187
June	Transitions	175	203
July	Relationships	149	193
August	Music	135	199

An ongoing challenge with training sessions is that the people who need them the most are the least likely to attend. For that reason, give major attention to how you describe the event in your publicity. Clearly communicate the benefits of any training event. Consider names like Teacher Time Out, Meeting the Teaching Challenge, Teaching Techniques Your Children Will Love, Teachers at Work, Teacher Training to Go, The Art of Teaching, Teachers' Chat Session. (See p. 40 for sample training event headlines.)

Special Training Events: Every year provide at least one training workshop or conference for your teachers. You may take them to a local, regional or denominational convention or seminar. You may cooperate with one or more other churches in your area, or you may plan and conduct the event just for your own teachers.

Individual Training: Whether people attend the planned training events or not, whether they serve on a regular continuing basis or just a month at a time, there are many informal opportunities to assist them in doing a better job.

• Let them observe an experienced teacher in action.

• Review information provided in your teacher handbook, explaining the rationale and benefits of each item in the handbook (see information about handbooks on p. 36).

• Provide teacher-training articles (such as those in this book; see pp. 83-178), videos and books to use at home.

• Display miniposters (pp. 179-222) in classrooms, hallways and offices as reminders of key points about early childhood ministry. (These miniposters can also be made into transparencies for use in teacher-training meetings.)

• Send out newsletters to teachers on a regular basis. Provide a few practical teacher-training tips, along with any organizational information that needs to be communicated.

Meeting the Teacher Challenge

Teachers Time-Out

The Art of Teaching

Teacher Training to GO

Teachers at Work

Teaching Techniques Your Children Will Love

Teachers' CHAT Session

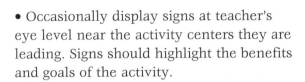

• Occasionally display signs at teacher's eye level near the activity centers they are leading. Signs should highlight the benefits and goals of the activity.

> ## THE ART CENTER
> *helps children*
> ♥ *learn to create*
> ♥ *enjoy the process of discovery*
> ♥ *express feelings and thoughts*

> ## THE GAME CENTER
> ### helps children
> → meet new challenges
> → use large muscles

> ## THE BLOCK CENTER
> ### HELPS CHILDREN
> ◆ LEARN TO MAKE DECISIONS
> ◆ PRACTICE SHARING AND COOPERATION

• Observe the person in action and then affirm every strong point (perhaps suggesting one or two specific ways to improve).

Regular Teachers' Meetings: It is important for teachers to meet together because of the spiritual, emotional and practical support they receive from each other. As teachers talk about their shared goals and strategies, they will increase their effectiveness and satisfaction. If problems exist, teachers can help each other improve their skills as they share successful ideas they have used. Perhaps the biggest benefit of teachers meeting together, however, is in the increased ability of teachers to meet the needs of children as they share insights and concerns about the children they teach.

A good meeting requires:

• advance publicity (church bulletins, postcards, posters at church, etc.) stating the reason for getting together;

• personal contacts by a leader to secure commitments to attend;

• provision for child care which does not burden the teachers;

• clearly defined starting and ending times on which people can depend;

• excitement over those who attend, not complaints about those who are absent;

• activities and discussion which focus on one or two topics that will help teachers improve their teaching;

• prayer for each other and the children and families in their classes;

• follow-up by leaders to inform any staff who were not present (consider a make-up meeting for people who have schedule conflicts).

During the meeting, you may want to provide some time for teachers who teach the same age level to meet together to choose responsibilities, plan materials and learn the suggested songs for upcoming lessons. Adapt the sample agenda on the next page as needed.

Meeting Agenda
(60-90 minutes)

5-10 minutes	Icebreaker activity
5 minutes	Welcome, prayer and announcements
20-30 minutes	Teacher training (watch video, discuss article, etc.)
15-20 minutes	Teachers' planning and sharing time
10-15 minutes	Devotional and prayer time
5-10 minutes	Refreshments

Thanking Teachers

Teachers involved in ministry to young children can never receive too much encouragement and appreciation. You can demonstrate in meaningful ways that your church places a high value on the people who volunteer their time and energy to teach young children.

• Thank-you gifts and cards can be given at the end of the school year or at the end of a teacher's term of service.

• Designate a Sunday at the beginning of each teaching term or program to dedicate or recognize those who will be teaching or helping in the coming days. Serve special refreshments and list teachers' names in the bulletin or a newsletter.

• Invite children and their parents to offer their thanks to teachers—homemade cards or treats.

• Plan an annual event to honor teachers.

Include the teachers and their spouses, family or other guests. These can be major events with decorations, special foods and entertainment; or they can be low-key and informal. The key is that they be well planned, communicating that someone thinks the teachers are important enough to have gone to some trouble on their behalf.

• Award certificates are another way in which churches show their appreciation to teachers.

Questions and Answers

 We'd like to use teenagers as part of our staff. What guidelines do we need to know?

 Many churches have planned effective ways of training and using youth in their early childhood ministries—always as helpers and never as teachers by themselves. Here are some guidelines for setting up a youth helper program:

First, determine with your church staff and youth leaders the minimum age and grade level for youth helpers and any other needed requirements, such as parent's permission to participate, regularly attend church youth classes and worship services, attend a specified number of training classes and be recommended by a youth supervisor/leader in the church. Ask youth to complete the volunteer application form (adapt form on pp. 31-32).

Second, plan one or more training classes for potential youth helpers and their parents. Including parents in the classes is helpful not only because it acquaints the parents with what their children are doing, but it also encourages parents to follow up at home on the training.

At the training classes, provide job descriptions and explain classroom procedures and safety guidelines. Emphasize that the job of a youth helper is an important task because of the way in which early experiences influence young children and because of the service youth helpers provide to the church family. Clearly state to helpers how important it is that they focus on children, not on other helpers in the room.

 In my church the Sunday School and worship service meet at the same time. The adults don't want to miss worship services, so how can I recruit teachers to serve on a regular basis?

If there are duplicate worship services being offered, a teacher can teach Sunday School one hour and attend church the next (or vice versa). If not, however, it is best to recruit a team of teachers for each class. Plan schedules to overlap so that some continuity is established from week to week (see sample schedule on this page).

If teachers must teach on a less than regular basis, encourage them to meet together regularly in order to plan learning activities and to establish a consistent class schedule and classroom procedures.

For the Sundays on which a teacher is unable to attend the worship service, provide a bulletin and, if possible, a recording of the service.

Schedule

Week 1	Teacher B	Teacher A
Week 2	Teacher A	Teacher C
Week 3	Teacher C	Teacher D
Week 4	Teacher D	Teacher B

 What should I do when teachers don't get along?

Occasionally, you may find that for one reason or another, the teachers in a particular class do not develop a friendship and find it difficult to work together. First, try to determine if there is an outside factor that could be causing the problem (one teacher always comes late, too many children for the number of teachers, etc.) and try to correct that problem. Second, consider adding a teacher to the team (sometimes a third party can help smooth out a relationship) or switching teaching assignments (one of the teachers may have a preference for another age level).

 How can I get my teachers to try something new?

Continuing to teach the way they've always taught is a common pattern for most people. The best way to encourage a teacher to try a new activity, practice a new skill or modify a class schedule is to provide the teacher with an opportunity to observe the new activity, skill or schedule in action. You may find that the teachers in one class are more open to making a change than other teachers. Begin with that class and then invite other teachers to observe it.

It is also easier to begin something new at the start of a new school year or new teaching term. Whether it is a new check-in procedure, a new class schedule or a new curriculum, clearly communicate to all of the teachers (and parents if needed) what is being changed and what benefits will result.

  What can I do when someone volunteers to teach, but I am unsure of how well he or she is suited to early childhood ministry?

Personally talk with the person if you do not already know him or her. Then if you feel the volunteer would be an asset to your program, ask the person to complete the volunteer application form you have developed. After the form has been completed, you may wish to place the volunteer alongside a long-term teacher who can help you observe the volunteer.

If you feel after personally interviewing the volunteer that he or she would not be suitable for your ministry, offer some tasks that will enable the volunteer to serve in another capacity (preparing lesson materials or bulletin boards, shopping for supplies, etc.).

  How can I get my teachers to arrive on time?

Some teachers find it difficult to get to their classes on time. Begin by making sure that all teachers are aware of what time they are expected to be in their classrooms. (Job descriptions should include a starting time.) Explain the benefits of having well-prepared teachers

present when children arrive (children feel welcome and can immediately begin learning) and the likely consequences when teachers are not present (children and parents feel unsure about who is in charge and children often begin playing with items not intended for their use).

If some children (other teacher's children, etc.) arrive much earlier than others, plan one or more rooms where they can be supervised while participating in several unstructured activities (watching a video, free play, coloring, etc.).

  What should I say when a parent wants to teach his or her own children in Sunday School?

Sometimes a parent will express a preference for teaching in his or her child's class. Serving as an occasional substitute or helper in the child's class may work out fine. Often, however, a child at the early childhood level finds it difficult to understand the parent's role in the classroom and the child frequently behaves in an entirely different manner when the parent is present. Normal interaction with other children suffers.

While helping parents understand the difficulties in teaching their own child's class, suggest ways parents can be helpers in their child's class: preparing materials, providing snack, etc. It's also good to encourage parents to teach in a class of children similar in age to their own children. Parents benefit greatly by seeing typical behavior patterns and seeing how skilled teachers interact with children. Some parents find it helpful to teach the next older age as a way to prepare for their own child's growth. Others feel more comfortable teaching the next youngest age, using experience gained from their child at that age.

How can I prepare for last-minute teacher substitutions?

When recruiting teachers, try to develop a list of people who will be on call as last-minute substitutes. Often, people who teach children during the week but who don't wish to teach regularly on the weekend make excellent substitutes because of their knowledge of children and experience in guiding classroom activities.

Periodically, administrative leaders can benefit by substituting. Teaching or helping in a class from time to time is essential to stay in touch with practical needs.

If you are unable to provide a substitute, a parent may be asked to lead or help in the classroom. Children may also be placed in nearby classes with children of similar ages (provided the teachers of those classes have room in their classes, have enough materials and agree to the change ahead of time).

Provide the substitute with a copy of the schedule and lesson for each class and a list of children's names. If name tags are not already available, make them for each child to wear. Also make sure that all supplies are readily available. If you are unable to provide the substitute with the appropriate lesson plan, be prepared in advance by having a generic lesson or two planned along with the supplies that are needed. Store the lesson and supplies in a "substitute box."

One of my teachers continually says her class is difficult or out of control. What can I do to determine specific ways to help her?

Ask the following questions to plan ways of improving the situation:

1. Is the number of teachers appropriate for the size of the class? Look at the chart of recommended teacher/child ratios on page 21. You can "handle" a group of children with fewer teachers, but the results are that teachers often spend much of their time in crowd control or in solving discipline problems.

2. Are the teachers present consistently so that relationships are being built and consistent classroom procedures are being followed?

3. Are the classes offering enough variety of learning activities? Is the class schedule designed to meet the needs of active children? You may need to sit in and observe the class in order to fully answer these questions. When children are being expected to act in ways beyond their age (for example, sitting still for extended periods), problems often result.

4. Are children being offered choices? Allowing children to make some of their own choices (which learning activity to participate in first, whether to use markers or crayons, what to build with the blocks, etc.) will help avoid discipline problems. Children's behavior is more positive when they are doing something they have chosen.

5. Does the problem behavior happen only at a certain time, such as when children first arrive or during the large-group Bible story time? If so, teachers can change procedures during the difficult time. For example, make sure teachers are present and prepared when children first arrive so that children are immediately involved in an appropriate activity, or have teachers

sit among children during large-group times, so they can redirect children's attention if needed.

6. Does the child need one-on-one supervision? For some children who consistently struggle with appropriate behavior, it may be helpful to ask an adult volunteer to participate in classroom activities alongside the child, building a friendship with the child and being available to redirect the child's behavior as needed.

7. Does the teacher need additional training? It may be helpful to ask the teacher to observe a more experienced teacher or to participate in one or more training meetings or conferences.

 When is the best time to schedule teacher-training meetings?

Talk with several leaders and teachers to determine the best time for teachers to meet. Consider the following possibilities:

• Week nights when the church calendar is relatively free of other meetings

• During the class time when teachers are already planning to be present (obtain parent substitutes for classes and provide simple activities for children during the class)

• At a Saturday morning brunch

• Immediately after the class time and/or worship service (offer a lunch to teachers and families and provide childcare for children during the meeting)

• At two different times, offering the same training and inviting teachers to choose the time that is best for them

Refer to pages 41-42 for more information on how to schedule and lead training meetings.

 What should I say when a parent wants to know if an older sibling can stay and be a helper in a younger child's class?

If the younger child is new to your church, you may want to invite the older child to stay and assist in the class for a week or two. Then explain to the parent "It was fun to get to know your daughter, but the activities in the class aren't designed for her. She will have a better time and learn more in a class for her own age. I'll be glad to introduce you to her teacher."

In general a good rule of thumb for teen helpers is for a separation of about 10 years to exist between preschoolers and helpers. If helpers and children in a classroom are too close in age, the teachers often find that the helper's "help" is minimal. (It is recommended that nursery helpers be at least 12 years old.)

Facilities and Supplies

What kind of place do the young children in your church need to help them learn important truths about God? Obviously, insights about God may come to a person in any setting. God is never limited by our physical surroundings. However, God did create young children with certain physical and learning characteristics that we need to take into careful consideration when planning the rooms in which they are taught. While your facilities need not be perfect, it is important to evaluate them regularly and make whatever improvements that are possible.

Young children work, play and learn with their whole bodies. They require rooms equipped for action. Open space, child-sized equipment and safe interesting materials make children feel their rooms at church are a good place to be. When children feel this way, teachers can effectively accomplish their Bible teaching ministry.

In addition, when class-rooms are inviting in their appearance, recruit-ing teachers and helpers is made easier. Staff who feel frustrated by poorly organized supplies or crowded conditions are not likely to return.

Space Requirements

Young children need to move, and movement requires space. Each person in attendance (children, teachers and helpers) needs a minimum of 25 to 35 square feet (2.25 to 3.15 sq. m) of space. Multiply the number of children in your room by 35 (or 10.5). Your answer represents the number of square feet (or meters) your room should contain. In order to accommodate varying attendance patterns, future growth, the needs of up to 20 to 24 active young children and their teachers, plus the use of rooms by multiple programs, it is recommended that all early childhood classrooms have at least 800 to 1,000 square feet (72 to 90 sq. m).

To determine how many children a room can adequately handle, first measure the length and width of your room. Multiply these two measurements. Divide the answer by 35 (or 10.5). Once each year (usually several months before children are promoted into new classes), reevaluate room designations by considering the number of children and their ages. Assign classes according to the following chart:

Attendance/Space Recommendations

Ages of children*	Teacher to child ratio**	Maximum number of children per room
2-year-olds	1 to 3 or 4	12 to 15
3-year-olds	1 to 5	16 to 20
4-year-olds to kindergarten	1 to 6	20 to 24

*If you combine ages, use the figures for the youngest children present in the room.
**See pages 21-22 for more information on teacher/child ratios.

Keep in mind that young children are likely to be stressed by large groups (even with an adequate amount of space and an adequate number of teachers). If your rooms are so large that more than 20 children are cared for in each room, consider ways of using sturdy dividers or other furniture to create smaller areas of space within the room.

Room Guidelines

Location: The ideal location for all early childhood classrooms is at ground level, with quick and easy access to a safe outside area and to restrooms. Avoid locating early childhood classrooms near the parking lot or busy streets. Rooms on the first floor allow efficient safety precautions as well as convenience for parents. When teachers take children outdoors, they can do so with a minimum of confusion.

Make sure classrooms are clearly marked and that ushers, greeters and the welcome/information-center staff know the location for each age level. Large churches often provide a labeled facilities map to direct parents to the appropriate rooms in which their children are cared for. A small church may post a white board on an easel near an entrance or at a central gathering area.

Floor Covering: Select a floor covering that is durable and easy to clean. Vinyl linoleum in a subdued pattern is usable for many activities. Washable carpeting provides a quiet, relaxed atmosphere, helping to control sound. Many churches combine linoleum and carpet in one room so that messy activities can be done over linoleum and there is also a comfortable area for being seated on the floor. If the entire floor is linoleum, provide carpet squares on which children may sit for large-group times. (Note: Cleaning materials for all kinds of surfaces must be easily accessible.)

Ceiling, Walls and Windows: Acoustical ceilings deaden sounds. Walls also should be insulated to block sound and be furnished with some sound-absorbing materials. Use wall paint that can be easily washed (usually semigloss). Windows of clear shatterproof glass, with the bottom sill two feet (.6 m) from the floor, provide children with a view of the outdoors (helpful when talking about items God has made). Securely fasten window screens. Window coverings should only be provided if needed to reduce glare and to insulate against heat or cold.

Lighting and Color: Lighting should be even and without glare in all parts of the room. Soft pastel colors help to create a warm, cheery atmosphere. To brighten rooms that are gloomy on darker days, use a soft yellow or pink wall color. To reduce glare in a sunny room, select pale blue or green colors. Bright colors can be added as highlights but should not overpower the room environment. (See Decorating Ideas on p. 58 for further guidelines on wall treatments.)

Toilet Facilities: Toilet facilities that immediately adjoin each room are desirable for children over two. A child-level sink and drinking fountain in each classroom are good investments.

Electrical Outlets: Electrical outlets equipped with safety plugs and out of children's reach should be provided on each wall to avoid the hazards of extension cords.

Room Temperature: Active young children need a room temperature between 68 and 70 degrees Fahrenheit (20 and 20.1 degrees Celsius). (Check the room temperature at child's level by hanging a thermometer about three feet [90 cm] from the floor.) If radiators or floor heaters are present, they must be covered. Adequate ventilation is also needed. A room of active children can get stuffy very easily, making children restless and uncomfortable.

Use the form on the next page to evaluate each of your early childhood rooms:

Room Evaluation Form

Class Name

Date _____

Evaluated by _____

Put an X in each box where improvement is needed

Room

The Classroom

Adequate space?					
Quick, easy movement from large to small groups?					
Adequate lighting from windows, fixtures?					
Proper ventilation?					
Controlled temperature?					
Floor and ceiling absorb sound?					
Bulletin boards/wall displays at students' eye level?					
Bulletin boards current and uncluttered?					
Electrical outlets accessible/adequate?					
Room attractively decorated?					
Walls clean, cheerful in color?					
Walls need repair/painting?					
Toilet, sink facilities easily accessible?					
Handicap access to room?					
Any doors that could be taken off small rooms to facilitate movement?					
Any walls that could be removed to give more flexibility?					
Adequate storage facilities?					
Floor coverings adequate, clean?					

Classroom Equipment

Furniture/equipment easily moved to provide flexibility?					
Classroom materials available, so students have easy access?					
Tables, chairs the right size?					
Any excess furniture that could be removed to provide more space?					
Any additional furniture/equipment needed?					
Any furniture/equipment needing repair/painting?					

Equipment and Furniture Needs

Consider these lists of equipment and furniture as ideals for which to strive—it may be overwhelming to think about providing all this equipment at once. Develop a set of priorities so that the most necessary things are purchased first. After you've obtained the basics, continue to evaluate the priorities of your classrooms, upgrading or adding equipment as your church budget allows.

In selecting equipment, it is often wiser to buy a few well-made items than many less expensive and less durable ones. Equipment of superior quality is well worth the investment in terms of years of hard wear. Regularly examine equipment and furniture for possible hazards such as cracks, splinters or missing parts.

Entrance Furniture: Cubbies or coatracks near each classroom's entrance are necessary pieces of equipment. The racks should include a place to store sweaters, coats, take-home projects, etc. for both children and adults. Coat hooks and a shelf can be mounted on the wall either in the room or in the hall outside your classroom door. A sign-in table or counter is helpful near the entrance. (See pp. 63-67 for more information on check-in procedures.)

Tables and Chairs: Young children learn best when they are comfortable. Tables and chairs in the correct sizes are essential for children to learn. Select chairs that are sturdy and not easily tipped over but are light enough for children to move. In early childhood classrooms, no adult-sized chairs are necessary, as teachers should sit at child's eye level. Tabletops should be durable and washable. Avoid large tables that seat more than six to eight. Select tables that allow the teacher to be within arm's reach of all children. Round tables have the advantage of having no corners, but rectangular tables are less expensive and are more efficiently used for art activities.

Recommended Sizes for Tables/Chairs for Ages 2 to 5

Chair: Height from floor+	10-14 inches (25.5-35.5 cm)*
Tables: 10 inches (25 cm) higher than chairs	20-24 inches (51-61 cm)
Tabletops: Durable and washable	Approx. 30x48 inches (76x122 cm)

+Stackable chairs are preferable.

*In early childhood rooms, no adult-sized chairs are necessary, as teachers should sit at child's eye level.

Storage Space: Ample storage space for each class is necessary. For teacher's materials, build cabinets mounted about 50 inches (127 cm) from the floor. Installation at this height frees the floor space below the cabinets, making more room for children's learning activities.

For displaying and storing children's materials and equipment, low open shelves have proven most successful. Place small items (Legos, toy cars, etc.) in transparent containers which fit on the shelves. Children can see what materials are available, can help themselves and then can return materials to the shelves. Bolt permanent shelves and cabinets to the wall. Small portable shelf units must also be sturdy enough that a child cannot tip them over. Avoid throwing classroom items into a bin. A box or a bin with materials piled in haphazardly is perhaps the poorest kind of storage unit. Children see chaos, rather than an orderly display of materials; and items can easily become lost, torn and soiled. Children often want to climb inside such a box or bin, making it a safety hazard.

If storage space in the classroom is limited, keep only basic supplies (glue, scissors, markers, crayons, etc.) in the classroom.

Additional supplies (construction paper, cardboard tubes, beanbags, etc.) can be kept in a central supply, or resource, room from which teachers obtain needed supplies on a weekly basis. Many larger churches find that it is more cost effective to maintain such a central storage area.

Make sure that each classroom has a designated space (cubby, table, clear floor area, etc.) for children to place take-home materials (activity pages, art projects, take-home papers, etc.) during the session. Some churches provide a labeled paper bag for each child to use for carrying materials home. Labels include the child's name and the lesson's Bible verse. Children may decorate the labels when they first arrive in the classroom.

Equipment for Bible Learning Activities: Active children need to participate in a variety of Bible learning activities, and they need the proper equipment to do it. Use the following supply list for the learning activities in your early childhood ministry:

Basic Materials

Art Center
- Newspaper or plastic tablecloth (to protect surfaces)
- Child-sized scissors
- Glue bottles and sticks
- Markers
- Crayons and chalk
- Tape
- Play dough
- Discarded magazines and catalogs
- Collage materials (yarn, ribbon, cotton balls, chenille wire, etc.)
- Construction paper in a variety of colors
- Stapler and staples
- Paint smocks (or old shirts)
- No-rinse hand-wiping solution, premoistened towelettes or paper towels
- Butcher paper

Blocks/Construction Center
- Wooden, plastic or cardboard blocks in different sizes, shapes and colors
- Toy cars and trucks
- Toy people and animals
- Stand-up traffic signs
- Recyclable materials (cardboard sheets, boxes and tubes; film canisters; wooden spools; etc.)
- Manipulative building toys (Legos, Lincoln Logs, etc.)

Dramatic Play Center
- Toy dishes, utensils, pans, bowls
- Tablecloth and/or place mats
- Plastic telephones
- Dolls (with rubber molded heads) and doll clothes and bedding
- Dress-up clothes (male and female) and accessories (purses, wallets, etc.)
- Full-length mirror
- Home-living furniture (kitchen appliances, rocking chair, etc.)
- Bible-times clothing (fabric strips for headbands and belts, fabric pieces with neckholes for tunics)

Game Center
- Beanbags
- Several soft balls in various sizes
- Masking tape (or painter's tape) and yarn
- Colored construction paper

- Scissors
- Butcher paper
- Markers

Music Center
- Rhythm instruments
- Children's music cassettes/CDs and player
- Art supplies (to make instruments as needed)

Nature/Science Center
- Several magnifying glasses
- A variety of nature items (rocks, shells, living plants, sticks, etc.)
- Large tubs or shallow pans for water or sand exploration
- Fabrics in a variety of textures

Snack Center
- Premoistened towelettes, no-rinse hand-wiping solution and paper towels
- Measuring cups and spoons
- Bowls in a variety of sizes
- Several spoons and ladles
- Plastic or paper dinnerware (plates, bowls, cups, napkins, utensils, etc.)
- Recipe ingredients as needed

Room Arrangements

Having enough space and the appropriate furniture and supplies is only part of providing good facilities. How the furniture is arranged in the room has a significant impact on a teacher's ability to involve children in active participation. In general, early childhood classes need a choice of activity areas/centers for part of the session and an area to come together for singing, story time, etc. during another time period.

Your room does not need to be completely or perfectly furnished for effective learning to begin. Once you staff a room with several loving, concerned teachers and a few pieces of basic equipment for children's firsthand learning experiences, you're ready for action. Organize furniture to form several separate areas, or centers. Equip each area to facilitate the kind of learning that will take place there.

Learning centers make it possible for children to use the appropriate materials without interfering with children involved in other activities. In addition, a shy child or one who is accustomed to working alone can participate more easily in a small area with a clearly defined focus and not be intimidated by having to relate to many other children. The outgoing child who is easily overstimulated can also work productively in a room arranged into centers.

Clearly defined activity areas help children stay constructively occupied in one learning area at a time.

In determining your room layout, keep in mind these safety guidelines:

• Arrange furniture so that there are no hard-to-supervise blind spots.

• Bolt shelves and cabinets to the wall.

• Attach safety hinges to doors, so they open and close slowly, preventing caught fingers or toes.

• Place furniture away from windows, protecting children who may climb on it.

• Evaluate the ways in which children will move from one area of the room to another, making sure that movement is not impeded.

• Do not block any entrance, exit or adjacent hallways with unused furniture. Every exit should be clearly marked. Contact your local fire department or state-licensing agency to help you determine proper placement of fire extinguishers, fire alarms, emergency exits and other safety considerations. (For example, all doors, even when locked, should be operable from the inside.) Post fire and other emergency (tornado, storm, earthquake, etc.) plans in every classroom, preferably by an exit door.

• When children are present in the room, do not stack chairs on tables.

• Check with your local fire department before hanging items from the ceiling. Moving ceiling tiles is sometimes a violation of fire safety codes.

Adapt the room arrangements on pages 53-55 to your facilities. Avoid creating rooms too small to be flexibly used as the needs of your early childhood ministry change over the years.

Since welcoming and checking in children are important aspects of early childhood ministry, carefully plan how your church will handle these procedures (check-in options are described on pp. 63-67).

Room Diagram for Twos to Fives

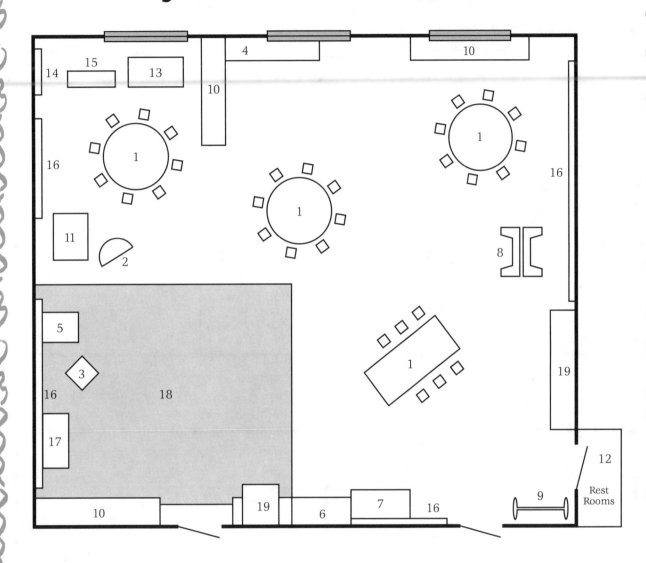

1. Table
2. Child rocker
3. Chair
4. Book rack
5. CD/cassette player
6. Storage cabinet and sink counter
7. Low supply table
8. Chalk/painting easel
9. Coatrack
10. Open shelf
11. Doll bed
12. Rest room
13. Child stove and sink
14. Wall mirror
15. Dress-up clothes
16. Bulletin board
17. Small table for teacher's materials
18. Rug
19. Shelves/table for take-home materials

Note: Rectangular rooms provide maximum flexibility.

Floor Plan Options

More than Two Rooms

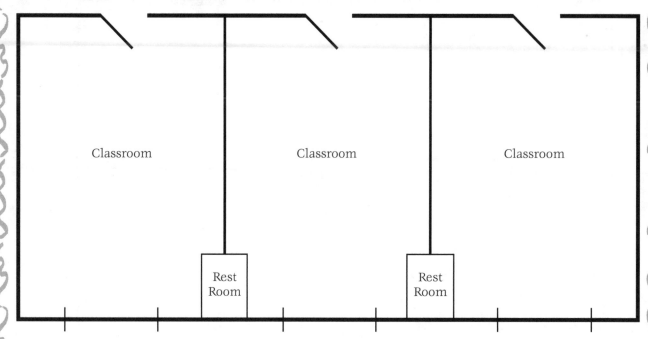

Classroom   Classroom   Classroom

Rest Room   Rest Room

Classroom and Playground

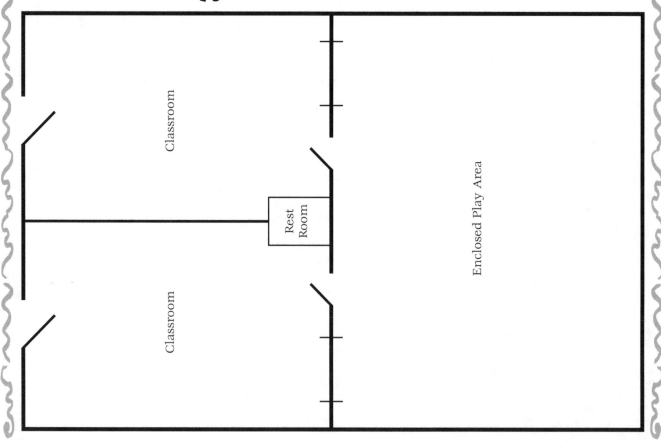

Classroom

Rest Room

Enclosed Play Area

Classroom

Floor Plan Options

Multiroom

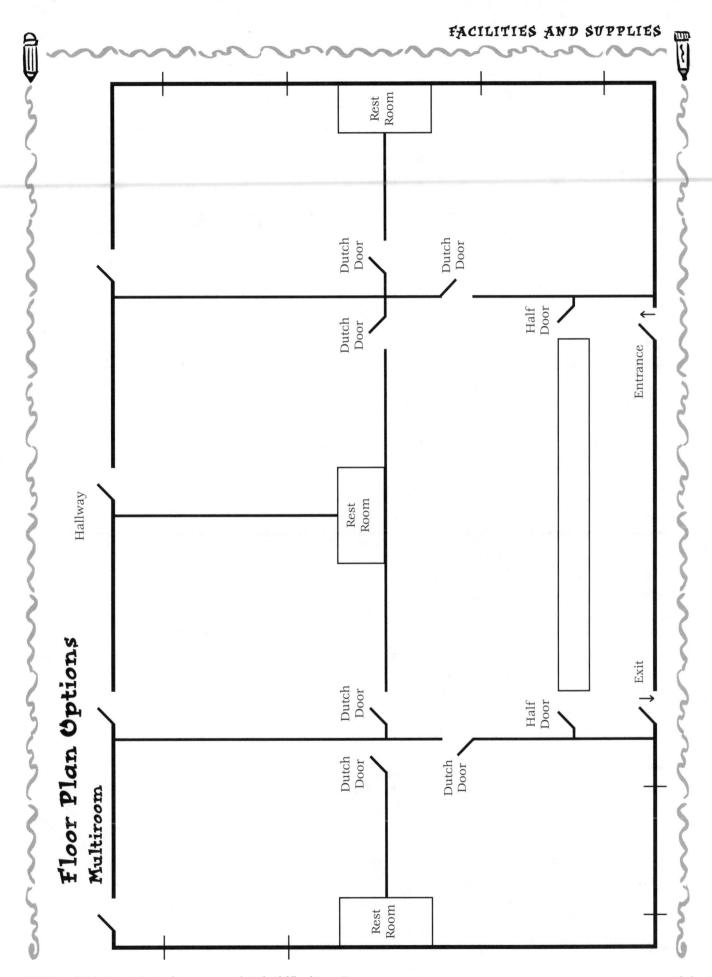

Hallway

Rest Room

Rest Room

Rest Room

Dutch Door

Dutch Door

Dutch Door

Dutch Door

Dutch Door

Half Door

Half Door

Entrance

Exit

Supply Room

A supply, or resource, room stocked with supplies, audiovisual equipment and curriculum resources should be readily accessible to all classroom areas. Most teachers are unlikely to walk very far to pick up items before class, so a large facility may need more than one such room. (Some churches provide coffee and snacks for their teachers in the supply, or resource, rooms as a way to build friendships and interaction among teachers.) A well-maintained supply room frees up classroom space and makes the job of teachers and helpers easier.

Maintain an up-to-date alphabetical list of the items (and their locations) stored in the supply room. Storing items in labeled clear plastic boxes makes it easy to see what's in the box as well as when there is a need to purchase additional items. Small containers such as ice-cream buckets can be kept in the supply room for teachers to use in collecting items and returning unused items. An individual who is unable to teach on Sunday mornings may be willing to serve as the coordinator of the supply room (see job description on p. 25).

Inform teachers regularly about new additions to the supply room. If there are certain kinds of activities you wish to encourage teachers to do, be sure that the supply room is well stocked with the needed supplies. Periodically ask several of your regular teachers to suggest frequently used items that could be added to your supply room. Adapt the list on page 57, giving a copy to each teacher and displaying it prominently in the supply room.

Depending on your church's procedures, you may allow teachers to purchase classroom supplies (set a maximum amount that can be purchased without prior approval) and then turn in receipts for reimbursement. You may also choose to use supply request forms which teachers must turn into you at least a week before the supply is needed (see sample supply request form below).

Supply Request

Date

Name and Phone Number

Class

What do you need?

How many do you need?

When do you need it?

Comments

Children's Ministries Supply List

Aluminum foil

Art foam

Autoharp

Baby food jars

Baggies

Balloons

Balls (foam, play-ground, tennis)

Beads

Beanbags

Beans

Bedsheet (for floor)

Burlap

Burlap sacks

Butcher paper rolls (brown, white, various sizes)

Buttons

Cardboard sheets

Cardboard tubes (toilet paper, paper towel)

Catalogs (discarded)

CD/cassette player

Cellophane tape

Chalk (white, colored, sidewalk)

Chenille wire in assorted colors

Chimes (tone, handheld)

Clothespins

Coffee cans (various sizes)

Coffee filters (white)

Confetti (in a variety of shapes)

Construction paper (in various sizes and colors)

Cotton balls (white, colored)

Cotton swabs

Craft sticks

Crayons

Crepe paper streamers

Extension cords

Fabric scraps

Farm animals

Felt

Film canisters

Flowers (plastic, silk)

Foil pie tins

Food coloring

Glitter

Glitter glue

Glue (large refill, small bottles, sticks)

Hole punches (handheld)

Index cards (large, small, white, colored, lined, unlined)

Jingle bells

Leaves (fall, artificial)

Magazines (discarded)

Magnifying glasses

Markers

Masking tape (wide, narrow)

Measuring sticks

Muffin cups

Nature items (rocks, feathers, shells, pinecones, pebbles)

Newspaper

Oatmeal containers

Offering container

Paint (watercolors, liquid tempera)

Paint smocks (or old shirts)

Paintbrushes

Painter's tape

Paper bags (grocery, lunch-sized)

Paper clips

Paper fasteners

Paper plates (large, small)

Pasta shapes

Pencils

Picture file (Bible stories, animals, nature, food, people)

Pinecones

Play dough and tools and cookie cutters

Poster board

Puppets

Raffia

Resealable bags in various sizes

Rhythm instruments

Ribbon (curling)

Rope

Rubber bands

Rulers

Safety pins (large, small)

Salt

Scarves

Scissors (adult-sized, child-sized)

Scratch paper

Seeds (a variety)

Shells

Stamps and stamp pads

Staplers and staples

Starch

Stickers (stars, happy faces, hearts, etc.)

Strawberry baskets

Straws

String

Tablecloths (plastic)

Thumbtacks

Tissue paper

Tongue depressors

Toothpicks

Trim

Twine

Utensils (plastic knives, spoons, forks)

Wallpaper samples

Waxed paper

Wiggle eyes

Yarn

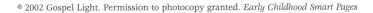

Decorating Ideas

Bulletin-board space in each classroom is desirable for displaying posters and children's artwork. Hang bulletin boards 18 inches (45 cm) from the floor. If possible, one bulletin board should be placed as a backdrop in the area where children gather for Bible story time so that Bible story pictures and other lesson-related items can be displayed.

Avoid cluttering the walls with unnecessary decorations. When too many pictures and objects are displayed on the walls, it becomes difficult for children to focus on the lesson-related items displayed. While nature or Bible-related murals can be attractively painted onto classroom walls, limit murals to no more than one wall in a classroom so that ample space remains for lesson-related items. Keep in mind that murals limit the flexibility of a room, making its use by more than one age level or other programs such as Vacation Bible School difficult. Also, children (and teachers) respond positively to new and fresh decorations. No matter how attractive, a

mural tends to be overlooked after initial interest has waned.

Display all items at children's eye level. Change items frequently (at least once a month) so that children are interested to see what is new in their classrooms.

Guidelines for Sharing Facilities

Rarely does any group have the luxury of being the only people to use a room. In many churches, most rooms are used frequently throughout the week. By following certain guidelines, you can help your staff share their rooms.

Guideline One: As often as possible, assign rooms for use by groups of the same or similar age. Establish a plan for scheduling use of the classrooms. Changes in schedule should be approved and communicated to all teachers involved.

Guideline Two: At least once a year, schedule a meeting with the teachers or leaders of the different groups that use a room. Allow time for each person to describe what his or her group does and the reasons why certain facility issues are important. When people meet together and talk about the goals of their programs, they become more accommodating to each other's needs. Help the people who share a room come to an agreement on what furniture, equipment and supplies will be shared and what will have restricted use. Establish guidelines for the use of shared resources. Discuss how each group is to leave the room for use by the other; then clearly communicate the guidelines to all staff who use the room. If the staff teach or lead the same age level, offer training to the teachers and leaders at the same time. (If you are unable to schedule a time when users of shared facilities can meet together, the leaders of each program should meet and develop a plan for sharing, which is then communicated to all who share the space. Large churches find it helpful to create a master plan for room setup in order to cut down custodial work.)

Guideline Three: Provide adequate storage space for each group's supplies. If this cannot be done in (or immediately nearby) the room, provide portable storage containers (available at office supply stores) for transporting needed items from a storage area. (See pp. 50-51 for more information on storage.)

Guideline Four: Provide appropriate display space for each group. It's important for each class or group to have something displayed that's focused on their interests. Assign specific display space in a room to each group that regularly uses the room. Portable bulletin boards can be rolled or carried into a room when needed. Build hinged boards that can easily be turned from one side to the next. Mount displays on butcher paper that can be attached to classroom walls for display and then rolled up for storage. If possible, request that any displays be limited to seasonal art that is then appropriate for all groups using the room.

Guideline Five: Plan for adequate custodial help to handle movement of furniture and equipment to prepare a room for use by different groups. Each group should provide the custodian with a clear diagram of how the room should be set up. If paid custodial help is not able to handle room setup on a regular basis, enlist volunteers to do the job so that teachers are not burdened with the task. You may also wish to post the room diagrams on classroom walls so that other groups who use the classrooms know how the room is to be arranged after their use.

Guideline Six: Develop creative solutions for seemingly unsolvable problems. For example, move a portable divider in front of stacks of unsightly desks or adult chairs or drape them with colorful fabric. One or two adult chairs can be used as a supply shelf for the materials needed by a class of young children.

Guideline Seven: If classrooms are used by a preschool, it is helpful to develop written guidelines for issues such as rent, storage, repair, maintenance, standards for use of rooms, etc. When staff changes occur at the church or at the preschool, review and update the guidelines. It is often helpful if one or more members of the church serve on the preschool board and if preschool parents and church members cooperate in facility cleanup projects.

Outdoor Play Areas

An outdoor play area for young children is a great resource for meeting children's need to move (and to make noise!). While a child's time at church will include much more than outdoor play, there is a great benefit in children being able to connect their enjoyment in play with the people and places where they learn about God. As children enjoy supervised outdoor playtime, they build friendships with each other; and teachers are able to informally build relationships with children, improving their ability to communicate God's love in everyday life.

The recommended space for a play area is 75 square feet (6.75 sq. m.) of outdoor space for each child. Outside play schedules can be staggered so that the area is not overcrowded.

Consider the following guidelines for your outdoor play area:

 **Guideline One: Completely fence in the play area.**

 **Guideline Two: Provide soft surfaces (grass and sand) as well as a hard surface (smooth cement is preferred over rough concrete or asphalt) for a variety of play experiences.** Avoid slippery surfaces such as gravel. Tripping hazards should be removed.

 **Guideline Three: Locate sand play areas in an area of the outdoor space farthest from classroom entrances so**

that sand brought indoors on children's feet and clothing is kept to a minimum.** It is best if sandboxes are covered when not in use so that animals are kept away from the sand.

 **Guideline Four: Plan for shade (awning, overhang, leafy tree, etc.) for at least a portion of the outdoor area.** Make sure trees and plants are not poisonous.

 **Guideline Five: Purchase age-appropriate equipment from educational supply stores and display a sign telling the ages for which each play area is designed.** Developmentally correct equipment for preschoolers includes small slides, low platforms, spring rocking equipment, crawl tunnels, playhouses and sand and/or water tables.

While it may be possible for church volunteers to build playground structures, safety standards must be strictly adhered to for the safety of the children and to protect your church from liability in case of injuries. For example, there should be no protruding bolts, or hooks around which children's clothing may become entangled, and there should be no sharp points or edges, which may injure children.

Equipment should offer as much variety as possible (climbing, sliding, crawling, etc.). Never allow children who are too old or too young to play on playground equipment. Pay special attention to the surface underneath playground equipment. For safety, sand areas need a minimum depth of 12 inches (30.5 cm) of loose fill. If properly installed, rubber tiles, hardwood fiber/mulch and safety-tested rubber mats are also options for playground surfaces. Safety surfaces should extend 6 feet (1.8 m) in all directions from playground equipment. Spaces that could trap children (between climbing rungs, etc.) must measure less than 3½ inches (9 cm) or more than 9 inches (23 cm). Guardrails and protective barriers should be a least 29 inches (73.5 cm) high. Make sure that all playground equipment is regularly inspected and maintained by adults who are knowledgeable in playground safety. When returning from outside play, provide opportunity for children to wash their hands.

Guideline Six: Outdoor play toys (balls in varying sizes, jump ropes, hula hoops, sand shovels and buckets, etc.) will encourage young children to develop large-muscle skills. Plan for adequate storage for these items, so they will remain in good condition.

Guideline Seven: Carefully supervise all outdoor play. Adults should look for potential hazards, guide children in safe use of equipment and be available in case of injury. Encourage teachers to be involved with children as they play, rather than using the time for adult conversation.

(Note: Free information regarding recommendations for outdoor play areas are provided by both state and federal agencies and are available on the Internet. If your church has a preschool or day-care facility, consult with your state's licensing agency for safety standards and the need for inspection by playground specialists.)

Questions and Answers

 We don't have a sink in any of our classrooms for young children. What can we do?

 When a room has no sink, plastic dishpans can be used for activities requiring water. If needed for washing hands, fill dishpan approximately halfway with slightly warm soapy water. You may also provide a commercial no-rinse hand-washing solution, premoistened towelettes or paper towels.

 How should we handle unwanted donations?

 Many times churches become the recipients of donated castoffs. These materials may have been suitable for home play, but frequently are not appropriate in a group setting. Thank the donor, saying "We'll look it over and pass it on to other children if it is not something the children are able to use in our program." You may give unneeded donations to an organization which repairs toys for reuse by charitable groups. When asking for donated items, be very specific in describing the materials needed (for example, stuffed animals must be washable and in good condition). If any donated item is unsafe for use by children, it is best to discard the item.

Our facilities are old and difficult to use with young children. What tips would you suggest?

  We rent space from a local school. What can we do to provide teachers with the equipment and supplies they need?

• Evaluate the space for hazards. Classrooms for young children must be safe.

• To create more open space, remove walls or portions of walls, even if posts must be retained.

• Widen doorways or remove unneeded closets or hallways.

• If rooms are windowless, paint the walls and ceilings in light colors, with some bright highlights on doors, trim, furniture, etc. Ask a lighting consultant to meet with you and give suggestions for updating the lighting.

• Challenge the congregation to value improved teaching facilities. Typically, rooms that are seen and used by everyone take precedence over rooms that are used mainly by two-year-olds! Encourage your teachers to join with you in becoming advocates for investing in the right kinds of places to effectively teach children.

As much as possible, plan to conduct early childhood classes in the rooms that have the least amount of furniture so that the youngest children have the most space. It may be necessary to bring in several large rugs or blankets for children to sit on. Unless storage space is supplied at the facility, each classroom's supplies will need to be stored in portable boxes which teachers keep at home and bring with them each week. Some churches store such boxes in large trailers that are brought to the facility each week prior to setup. (Color-code the boxes for easy identification.) If possible, take advantage of any outdoor space available. Adapt the materials used in Bible learning activities as needed. For example, instead of children building with large cardboard or wooden blocks, they may build with smaller interlocking blocks or small alphabet blocks.

Health and Safety

Well-thought-out health and safety procedures benefit everyone in your early childhood ministry. Children are of course the prime beneficiaries. In a safe environment that is planned just for them, young children are encouraged to learn and grow. Secure in the knowledge that everything possible is being done to keep their child safe and happy, parents can take advantage of time away from their children to build their own relationships with God and others in the church family.

Teachers and helpers also find that making health and safety issues a priority makes their service a positive experience. For example, a church without a firm well-child policy may find their teachers (not to mention other children) frequently exposed to illnesses. Establishing guidelines for specific classroom procedures (checking in, restroom use, emergencies, etc.) also helps the staff to know and fulfill what is expected of them. Other safety guidelines (child/adult ratios, etc.) protect teachers in the event of a complaint.

In discussing health and safety procedures with teachers and parents, communicate instructions with a positive approach. "In order to help our program be the best it can be, these are the health and safety guidelines we follow" or "So that you can concentrate on teaching the children in your class, here are the health and safety procedures we've established." Post the guidelines in classrooms and frequently thank parents and teachers for their attention to these issues.

Occasionally a parent or teacher may question the need for a certain safety procedure. Acknowledge the person's feelings ("It does seem like it takes extra time to have parents sign in their children"), but reaffirm the need for such a procedure ("Making sure everyone signs in helps us keep children safe").

Health and safety guidelines are best developed with input from a number of people. Teachers, parents and lawyers familiar with church liability issues all can give valuable input. You may also request that a consultant from your state's Occupational Safety and Health Agency (OSHA) visit your facility to evaluate the facility for safety and health hazards. Some churches have found it helpful to create a committee which meets one or more times a year to evaluate and update as needed the health and safety guidelines.

Check-In Procedures

Every church needs to evaluate the number of children in its programs and decide if parents will be asked to check in their children at a counter or reception area, or if they may bring their children directly to individual classrooms. The size of your church and the number of children in your program will often determine the extensiveness of the check-in procedures you set up. However, some clearly stated procedures need to be established in any church so that each child is safe and protected. Safety guidelines also provide needed legal protection for teachers and helpers.

Registration Cards: At the beginning of the school year or whenever a new child joins your program, the child's parents should complete a registration card. Use names and addresses for maintaining home contacts (mailing birthday cards to children, sending invitations to special events, absentee follow-up, etc.).

A church may choose to ask a parent to

complete a more extensive registration form which includes name of family doctor, name of person who will care for child if parent cannot be reached, medical insurance information and liability release statements to be signed by the parent. If your church desires to use such a registration form, consult a book about church liability issues and/or contact a lawyer who is familiar with the laws in your state for help in designing a legal and appropriate form.

Adapt this sample card and the medical release form on page 65 for your own church. (Note: Some churches provide registration cards with space for all children in the family to be listed so that parents do not have to fill out multiple cards. Cards are then photocopied and distributed to each child's class.)

Sunday School Registration

Child's Name _____   Today's Date _____

Age _____   Gender _____   Birth Date _____

Address _____

City/State/Zip _____   Phone Number _____

Food Allergies (if any)

Father's Name (include address and phone number if different from above)

Mother's Name (include address and phone number if different from above)

Siblings' Names and Ages

Parent Participation: I would be willing to help with

_____ Snacks   _____ Games   _____ Art   _____ Music   _____ Drama

_____ Other _____

Medical and Liability Release Form

IMPORTANT: *This is a sample form, not intended to be reproduced. Adapt to your specific needs.*

Parent Permission/Release Form

(Church Name)

(Address)

(Phone Number)

Child's Name _____

Birth Date _____ Grade _____

Address _____

City _____ Zip _____

Phone Number _____

Date(s) of Activity _____

Authorization of Consent for Treatment of Minor

I, the undersigned parent or guardian of _____,
a minor, do hereby authorize any duly authorized employee, volunteer or other representative
of the (church name), as agent(s) for the undersigned, to consent to any x-ray examination,
anesthetic, medical or surgical diagnosis or treatment, and hospital care which is deemed
advisable by, and is to be rendered under the general or specific supervision of, any licensed
physician and surgeon, whether such diagnosis or treatment is rendered at the office of said
physician and surgeon or at a clinic, hospital or other medical facility.

It is understood that this authorization is given in advance of any specific diagnosis, treatment
or hospital care being required, but is given to provide authority and power on the part of our
aforesaid agent(s) to give specific consent to any and all such diagnosis treatment or hospital
care which the aforementioned physician in the exercise of his or her best judgment may
deem advisable.

This authorization shall remain effective from _____ to _____.

Signature _____

Check-In Forms: A typical check-in form asks for the child's name and age, parents' names and where they will be located. Parents sign the form when leaving and picking up their children. Encourage everyone, even your most regular attendees, to completely fill out these forms. Make the forms easier for parents to complete by reducing the amount of time it takes to fill in the desired information. For example, provide forms with children's names and ages already preprinted. Visitors add their names at the bottom of the list. You may also preprint the variety of locations where parents might be, asking parents to simply check off the appropriate locations.

4-Year-Olds Check-In   Date _____

Child's Name	Age of Child	Parent's Name	Write Your Location in Church Buildings				Sign-In Time	Sign-Out Time
			Sat. p.m.	Sunday 8:00	Sunday 9:15	Sunday 11:00		

Name Tags: Depending on the size of your church, you may choose to provide each child and teacher with a name tag. Blank tags should be made available for visitors. Even if name tags are not regularly used in a classroom, they can be helpful when a substitute is present. For younger children, affix the name tag on the child's back, so he or she doesn't pull it off.

Child and Parent Identification: Many churches have developed a system for child identification that ensures children's safety and that they are only released to approved adults. Teachers are then protected from parent complaints and from legal action in instances of custody disputes.

Consider these ideas for a child identification systems, choosing one that best fits your church. You can make your own tags or coupons (see samples on this page) or purchase commercially made child/parent identification systems. Contact your local Christian bookstore for possible sources.

• Coupon with Date and Child's Name— Coupon is given to parent when the child is checked in. Only the person with the coupon is allowed to pick up the child at the end of the session.

• Number ID—Card or paper with date and number assigned to the child. A tag with the corresponding number may also be attached to the child's nametag.

• Pagers—Numbered vibrating pagers are given to parents when their child is checked in. The child is dismissed to the parent when the pager is returned.

• Wallet-Sized, Permanent Identification Cards—These cards, with parents' and children's names and personal family identification number, can be given to parents. A child is only released to an adult who shows the identification card.

• Photo ID—Take photos of each child with his or her parents. Mount photos on a bulletin board near the entrance to each room.

Have an instant camera available to photograph visitors.

• Parent Designation—Provide a section on the check-in form in which the parent writes the name of the person who will be picking up the child. Person picking up the child would be requested to show identification if not known to the child's teacher.

Community Church
Children's Ministries

Name

_____

Number

_____

Date

_____

To protect your child, please return this coupon to the teacher when picking him or her up.

First Church
Child Security Tag

Date _____

This tag must be returned in order for your child to be released from the classroom.

We appreciate your cooperation!

Your child's number is _____.

Keeping Clean

Keeping things clean is always an issue of concern in any program involving children—especially one in which children spend a good deal of time on the floor and handling a variety of items. You may want to provide charts (adapt those on this page) on which to record cleaning assignments. (If you share facilities with a preschool or day-care program, coordinate cleaning with the leaders of those programs.)

• Plan which tasks will be done by teachers and which will be done by the custodian.

• Vacuum carpets or mop the floors after each day's use, cleaning up any spills immediately.

• Store all cleaning supplies out of reach of children, preferably in cabinets or closets that either lock or have safety latches.

• Schedule long-term cleaning tasks such as washing windows, curtains, blinds, shelves, chairs and large toy items. Shampoo carpets once a year.

One often-overlooked detail in keeping rooms clean is the leftover items that seem to accumulate in rooms. Sunday School papers, Bibles, hair clips, small toys, used coffee or punch cups, cookies, etc., often appear in rooms. Each teacher can be asked to dispose of such items in the trash or in a Lost and Found Box, or whoever is responsible for locking up classrooms can collect such items at the end of the session.

Daily Room Care

Today's Date _____

❑ Wash Tables

❑ Wash and Disinfect Toys As Needed

❑ Disinfect Furniture, Tables, Door Knobs and Light Switches

❑ Vacuum Rug and Mop Floor

❑ Spot Clean Spills

Long-Term Room Care

Room _____

MONTHLY _____

Date _____

❑ Wash Windows

❑ Wash Rugs

❑ Wipe Off and Disinfect Large Toy Items

SIX MONTHS _____

Date _____

❑ Wash Window Treatments

❑ Shampoo Carpet

YEARLY _____

Date _____

❑ Wash/Paint walls

Hand Washing

Frequent hand washing will do much to prevent the spread of infections. Encourage staff to wash their hands before beginning their teaching assignment, before handling food, after going to the bathroom, after helping a child with toileting, after any contact with body fluids and after cleaning equipment or supplies.

Wash hands with running water and antibacterial soap, rubbing front and back of hands together for 15 to 30 seconds. Dry hands with disposable towels. Use a disposable towel to turn off the faucet so that hands are not contaminated again. Display hand washing instructions (see below) near each sink.

Ask your teachers to plan time for children to wash hands before eating and after going to the bathroom.

If your classrooms do not have nearby sink facilities, provide a commercial no-rinse hand-washing solution, premoistened towelettes or paper towels for teachers and children to use.

Hand Washing Is the Best Prevention

Wash and wipe your hands together, live in health forever!

Take time to wash:

✓ when you first arrive

✓ before handling food

✓ after using the restroom

✓ after changing a child's diaper

✓ after any contact with body fluids

✓ after cleaning up

Everything you ever wanted to know about washing hands:

✓ wash with running water and antibacterial soap

✓ wash front and back of hands

✓ wash for 15-30 seconds

✓ turn off faucet with disposable towel

✓ dry hands with disposable towel

Illnesses

One of the most frequent concerns of parents whose children are in a group setting is whether or not the other children are healthy. Carefully plan how the health of children and staff is monitored.

The basic foundation for maintaining healthy classrooms is a well-child policy. Establishing, communicating and firmly adhering to a well-child policy will reassure parents. Communicate your well-child policy by including it in a parent handbook or brochure and in parent newsletters. Display well-child guidelines on parent bulletin boards or entry areas. At the beginning of the winter cold-and-flu season, many churches send home a letter reminding parents of health guidelines.

Ask teachers to do a quick visual health inspection as children are checked in to their classrooms. While some symptoms are not visible at a quick glance, a runny nose or frequent cough should prompt a conversation with the child's parents. Simply state in a friendly manner what you have observed and invite the parent's response. "I hear Megan coughing a lot. How does she feel today?" or "Daniel's nose seems to be running. How is he feeling? Does he have a cold?"

It's difficult to exclude a child from the class, but most parents will respond to a conversation that makes it clear the parents and teachers are a team working together for the child's health. "I'll ask Mrs. Jones to keep an eye on Kasey. If his runny nose continues, he'd probably feel more comfortable if you took him home." "The Children's Ministry Director has asked us to pay spe-

Good Health Guidelines

We want to provide a healthy environment in our classrooms, so we ask you to keep your child at home when any of the following have occured within the last 24 hours:

Fever/Vomiting

Discharge in or around the eyes

Green or yellow runny nose

Excessive coughing

Diarrhea

Questionable rash

Any communicable disease

If your child becomes ill while in the classroom, you will be notified promptly.

If your child is being treated with an antibiotic, he or she should have received treatment for at least 24 hours before coming to the classroom.

For your child's protection, we ask our teachers to follow these same guidelines.

Dear Parents of Preschoolers,

Young children are very susceptible to colds, flus and other diseases. We realize a child's illness can be a difficult time for a parent, and it's often frustrating to rearrange your schedules to provide care for a sick child at home.

We want to help eliminate these concerns as much as possible. This requires that our classrooms have the healthiest environment possible. The best way to prevent illness is to prevent exposure. The purpose of this letter is to help our teachers and parents work together to provide a healthy environment.

1. Please keep your child at home if any one of the following is true: your child has a fever or has had a fever in the past 24 hours; your child has vomited or had diarrhea in the past 24 hours.

2. A quick health check will be conducted when you bring your child to the classroom. A child will not be admitted with any of these symptoms: matter in the eyes, frequent coughing, runny nose (anything but clear discharge).

Thanks for letting us care for and love your child. Please do not hesitate to call if you have any questions or comments about our program.

Sunday School Coordinator

555-5555

cial attention to our well-child policy during this time of colds and flu. We're sorry, but it looks (or sounds) as if Abby would be better off at home today."

Occasionally a child has been determined to have allergies that cause a continual runny nose (clear discharge), rash or cough. Ask parents to alert you to allergies of this sort.

Encourage teachers to stay home when they are sick by having a ready list of substitutes. Don't hesitate to ask a teacher with symptoms of ill health to go home.

If a child has recently been ill and is no longer contagious but still receives medication, parents should administer the medication. (Medications brought by parents should be stored properly away from the reach of children, in a refrigerator if needed.)

Infectious Diseases

Children with infectious diseases such as mumps, measles, chicken pox, conjunctivitis and impetigo should be kept at home until all possibility of contagion is over.

The health and safety guidelines developed by your church should include guidelines for responding to children who have hepatitis (HBV) or AIDS or who may be HIV positive. Write procedures for handling these diseases in conjunction with church-wide guidelines. Include facts about the disease, information about the infection control procedures followed in your church (e.g., cleaning procedures, etc.) and confidentiality policies. A sample infectious disease policy and a related form are on the next two pages. Because laws about the treatment of people with infectious diseases are subject to change, it is best to consult a state health agency and a competent local attorney for further information about state and federal laws at the time you are developing your church's procedures and policies.

INFECTIOUS DISEASE/AIDS & HBV POLICY

STATEMENT OF PURPOSE

We commit ourselves to being knowledgeable and informed about infectious diseases/AIDS & HBV (Hepatitis B Virus) and to be a support network that is nonjudgmental, compassionate and Christ-centered, capable of providing spiritual and emotional support to those infected as well as affected family members and friends.

While we do not condone the behaviors that sometimes result in AIDS, we know Jesus loves every individual and desires for all to come to Him in repentance. We believe we are assisting God's work in the person's life when we extend compassionate care to infected people. It could well be that our loving ministry to an HIV-infected person is what will successfully communicate God's love to him or her.

MEDICAL FACTS ABOUT AIDS

Acquired Immune Deficiency Syndrome (AIDS) is a serious life-threatening condition. The best scientific evidence indicates that AIDS is caused by a virus known as HIV (Human Immunodeficiency Virus), which is transmitted through exposure to infected blood or semen through sexual contact, injury, sharing of contaminated needles, or from an infected mother to child before or around the time of birth. Not every infant who tests positive is actually HIV infected. One-half to two-thirds will be completely free from evidence of infection by eighteen months, after antibodies from the mother have dissipated from the infant's blood.

OUR RESPONSE

Any individual who has been diagnosed with any infectious disease and/or is HIV positive or has AIDS should be treated similarly to any other individual attending our church. In general, we will not reject or ostracize anyone who has an infectious disease, is HIV positive or who has AIDS as long as that individual presents no real threat to the safety of others in the congregation (example: open sores or inability to control bodily functions). Confidentiality regarding individuals who have infectious diseases or are HIV positive or have AIDS will be respected.

United States Public Health Service guidelines for infectious diseases will be followed for all individuals including infants and children in the Nursery, Sunday School and Day/After School Care. Nursery and Children's Workers and other appropriate groups will be trained accordingly, using universal precautions.

"Universal precautions" refers to the handling of body fluids from all students and not just those known to be infected with a blood-borne pathogen.

Universal precautions require the use of protective barriers such as gloves, protective eye wear, gowns and masks. Precautions beyond the use of gloves would only be required in unusual circumstances in the school setting. Gloves do not, however, prevent possible exposure due to penetrating injuries from needles or sharp instruments.

The AIDS Committee

A standing AIDS Committee will be established to help anyone in our congregation who is HIV positive. The committee will assess how the church can be most supportive of the person/family and will administer the guidelines of this policy to ensure that the patient's church experience is as good as the experience of any other church attender.

The specific duties of the committee include the following:

1. When a person identifies him-/herself or his/her child as HIV positive to anyone in the congregation, the person should be told about the AIDS Committee and encouraged to contact the chairman. The chairman will arrange for one or more committee members to visit with the person or family and assess the needs and desires of the patient.

2. One member, preferably a health-care professional, will volunteer to receive calls from anyone in the congregation who has a question or concern about AIDS. The person's phone number will be published in appropriate church publications.

3. The committee will meet on a case-by-case basis to talk to and help any family bringing an infected child to church. The committee or its representative will convey the goals of the church and initiate the procedures adopted for infected children.

Each case will be examined individually and flexibility maintained. The child's physician, parents or guardian, and the AIDS Committee will decide how to bring such a child to church.

While these decisions are being made, an adult will be assigned to personally minister to and monitor the HIV-infected child.

Toddlers and infants with HIV infection will be integrated slowly into the classroom. The child will begin in a playpen and an assigned monitor will stay with the child at all times. This monitor might initially be a doctor or nurse who would care for the child, keep his/her toys away from others, and change diapers. Later the monitor could be any responsible adult. (The close observation is not necessary to prevent transfer of HIV disease but to alleviate the anxieties of other parents.) Play outside the playpen and full integration into the class will depend on the child's behavior and the sentiment of the parents of the other children.

Infants through sixth grade children who are infected will be identified to the parents of the other children in the Sunday School class and to the Sunday School teachers. The AIDS Committee will be in charge of a concentrated communication and education effort with the desired effect of reducing anxieties and providing a quality church environment for the HIV-infected child. If the anxiety of the parents and other children is so high that the infected child is in danger of being ostracized, then the committee will find at least two people who can play with the infected child, teach the Sunday School lesson and serve him/her in every need.

EDUCATION FOR THE CONGREGATION

According to the most recent research data from the Center for Disease Control, "No documented cases of HIV infection have been traced to casual contact." Since knowledge can dispel fear and set the groundwork for compassionate understanding, we shall commit to educating the church regarding infectious diseases and HIV-related issues.

Protective Measures

The best way to prevent the spread of blood-transmitted infections such as HIV is to utilize "universal precautions," which means the blood of everyone is considered potentially infectious. Since the vast majority of people who have HIV are unaware of their infection, the greatest danger is exposure to the blood of an infected child or adult who is assumed to be uninfected. Therefore all blood spills will be handled with caution.

Latex examination gloves will be worn when contact is anticipated with blood, open sores, cuts or the inside of a person's mouth. Gloves will also be used when handling objects that are contaminated with blood. Children's workers with open sores on the hand will wear gloves. Open sores elsewhere on the body will be covered with an adequate-sized bandage.

Gloves will be readily available throughout the church. They will be stored in the nursery, in children's Sunday School rooms, in the kitchen and on the playground.

Since HIV is destroyed by household bleach, a solution of one part bleach to ten parts water will be kept in the first-aid cabinet. The bleach solution will be stored at room temperature in closed opaque plastic containers and made fresh at the beginning of each session. Small blood spills will be cleaned while wearing gloves, using disposable towels moistened with the bleach solution. If a large spill of blood occurs, the area will be cleaned with disposable paper towels or linens while wearing gloves. The bleach solution will then be poured over the area, and the area cleaned again.

PARENTAL RELEASE FORM FOR HIV POSITIVE CHILD

As a parents of _____

I do give my consent for a bona fide need-to-know person to be informed that my child is HIV positive so that she or he can be attended to in case of emergency.

_____
Signed

Accidents

Your early childhood staff need to be familiar with efficient procedures for handling accidents, even though they may never need to put the procedures into practice. Often, a quick hug and sympathetic ear are enough to calm a child's outward distress. However, teachers need to be watchful no matter how slight the injury appears and certain questions must be considered:

- Is the child unresponsive?
- Is the child having difficulty breathing?
- Is the child's cry unusual?
- Is the child's pulse weak or rapid?
- Is the child vomiting?
- Is the child's skin broken?

If any of these questions are answered in the affirmative, call for medical help and/or provide treatment immediately and call the parents.

Each classroom should have an up-to-date first-aid manual (available from your local American Red Cross agency) that is clearly in view and a first aid kit stored out of children's reach. Once a month check the kit contents and replace items as needed.

Staff should also have quick access to a telephone if emergency medical services are required. Post emergency phone numbers (9-1-1 or local hospital, police and fire departments and poison control centers) near each telephone, along with directions to your facility and to the building and/or room.

Consider these additional tips for handling accidents:

- During each session, designate a person in the building or on the premises who is trained in CPR for children. (Provide CPR and first aid classes for staff on a regular basis.)

- Never hesitate to offer first aid to an injured child, but wear disposable gloves while cleaning up blood or other bodily

Parent Notification

I Was Hurt Today (But I'm OK Now!)

Where I Was: _____

_____

What Happened: _____

_____

_____

_____ helped me by

_____.

fluids. Have gloves available at all times.

Any time a child sustains an injury, verbal and written reports need to be completed. (See forms on this and previous page.) Parents and a designated person on the church staff should be informed of the injury and the circumstances in which it occurred and how the injury was treated. (Follow any guidelines that have already been established by your church.) Follow up the injury with a phone call to the parents the day after the injury took place to determine if further injuries have developed and to express your care and concern for the child involved.

If a staff person, whether paid or volunteer, is injured while serving in ministry, follow the insurance and liability procedures your church has already established for employees and volunteer workers.

Church Office Notification Injury Report

Name, Age and Gender of Child Who Was Injured

_____

Address/City/Zip _____

Name of Parent _____ Phone Number _____

Date and Time of Accident _____

Describe in detail how the child was injured, including location, names and actions of all children and adults involved.

_____

_____

Describe the child's injuries and what action was taken to treat the injuries.

_____

How and when was the parent notified?

_____

Please list names and phone numbers of witnesses to the accident.

1. _____

2. _____

3. _____

Additional Comments _____

Your Name, Address and Phone Number _____

_____

Emergencies

All churches should have planned procedures in case of fire and/or emergency evacuation. Depending on your church's location, you may also need to provide information for emergencies such as earthquakes, tornadoes and floods. Ask your local American Red Cross agency to provide you with the appropriate posters and/or handouts to display or have on hand. Summarize pertinent emergency information at teacher training meetings or in a teacher handbook.

• Plan who will alert teachers to evacuate their classrooms.

• Plan and post two emergency exits from each classroom and have fire extinguishers on hand. (Ask your local fire department to help you determine the safest routes and where fire extinguishers should be mounted.) Designate a meeting place for all children and staff.

• Keep a bag of emergency supplies (snacks, disposable gloves, first-aid kit, flashlight, portable radio, water, etc.) elsewhere on the church premises, in a place quickly accessible to teachers in case of evacuation.

• Always have at least one working flashlight available in each classroom, in case of a power outage or if an evacuation takes place at night.

• Consider how teachers will communicate with each other and with parents in case of emergencies (phones, cell phones or walkie-talkies).

Child Abuse Prevention and Reporting

Developing safety procedures for preventing and reporting child abuse is somewhat like taking a CPR class. While never expecting to have a problem, it is wise to take necessary precautions. People who minister to children need to be trained to know how to respond if there is a situation calling for action, praying that it will not be needed.

Adapt the sample policy on pages 33-34 to help your church create a safe place for both children and adults in your early childhood ministry, which includes guidelines for teacher selection (see information regarding screening of volunteers on pp. 28 and 30) and teacher practices. In addition, inform your teachers of the definition of child abuse and the instructions for reporting it. All staff should be familiarized with these policies and instructions on an annual basis. (It is recommended that a lawyer evaluate your policies to be sure they conform to your state's laws regarding child abuse.)

How to Report Suspected Child Abuse

1. All teachers are to be familiar with the definitions of child abuse (see p. 77).

2. If a teacher suspects that a child in the church has been abused, the following steps are to be followed:

• Report the suspected abuse to your supervisor.

• Do not interview the child regarding the suspected abuse. The interview process will be handled by trained personnel.

• Do not discuss the suspected abuse. It is important that all information about the suspected child abuse (victim and abuser) be kept confidential.

3. Teachers reporting suspected child abuse will be asked to complete the Suspected Child Abuse Report (available from your state's Department of Social Services). Confidentiality will be maintained where possible. This report must be completed within 24 hours.

4. Once a suspected child abuse case has been reported by a teacher to a supervisor, it will be reported to the designated reporting agency.

Adapted by permission from Bible Fellowship Church, Ventura, California.

Definitions of Child Abuse

Defined by The National Committee for Prevention of Child Abuse

Physical Abuse: Nonaccidental injury, which may include beatings, violent shaking, human bites, strangulation, suffocation, poisoning, or burns. The results may be bruises and welts, broken bones, scars, permanent disfigurement, long-lasting psychological damage, serious internal injuries, brain damage, or death.

Neglect: The failure to provide a child with basic needs, including food, clothing, education, shelter, and medical care; also abandonment and inadequate supervision.

Sexual Abuse: The sexual exploitation of a child by an older person, as in rape, incest, fondling of the genitals, exhibitionism, or pornography. It may be done for the sexual gratification of the older person, out of a need for power, or for economic reasons.

Questions and Answers

What should we do if a child gets sick during class?

Sometimes a child develops symptoms of illness during a class session. The child may be in pain, appear lethargic, have a flushed face or sudden rash, cough frequently and sound congested, or exhibit discharge from the nose or eyes. If any of these symptoms appear, contact the parent and request that the child be taken home for his or her own comfort and health. Until a parent arrives to pick up the child, keep the child isolated in an area of the classroom.

How can we be prepared for bathroom accidents?

It is not uncommon for young children to occasionally forget to go to the bathroom in time. Treat bathroom accidents in a manner-of-fact way. "Cody, I see we forgot to take you to the bathroom on time. Let me help you clean up." In early childhood programs, it's a good idea to have one or more spare sets of clothing and/or pull-up diapers that can be used when children need a change of clothes. Thoroughly clean and disinfect the area where the accident happened.

We occasionally have problems with preschoolers biting. Everyone gets upset! What can we do?

With babies and toddlers, biting usually occurs because they are teething, they don't have the words to communicate frustration, or they just want to see what happens. With older children, however, biting may signify a deeper feeling of anger or aggressiveness.

When a child bites, take immediate action: (1) Separate the biter from the rest of the group. One adult should care for the bitten child, while another adult deals with the biter. Offer comfort and first aid if needed to the bitten child. Even if the bite did not break the skin, cleanse the area with antiseptic. Offer a bandage or a cold compress. (2) Talk to the child who bit. Firmly say, "Kelly, biting hurts. I can't let you bite. If you want to play with your friends, you must not bite. Let's sit here quietly for a while until you are ready to play again."

Then two additional steps need to be taken: (1) The child who has bitten needs to be closely supervised for the rest of the session and in succeeding sessions to be sure the biting behavior does not reoccur. If biting happens repeatedly, try to identify a pattern of circumstances that lead to biting. Then intervene before biting occurs. (2) A report (see the sample form below) should be made in writing to the parents of the children involved. Briefly describe the circumstances. Describe what treatment steps were taken and what was said

Parent Note

Date _____

_____ was bitten on

the _____

today in the _____ class.

The skin was ❒ not broken. ❒ broken.

We comforted and

   ❒ washed the bite.

   ❒ put an antiseptic ointment on the bite.

   ❒ placed a bandage on the bite.

   ❒ held a cold compress on the bite.

When a child is bitten in our Sunday School, we move the biter away from other children and gently but firmly instruct the child not to bite. We closely observe the child who bit in order to prevent any future occurrences. We also alert the parents of the child's behavior. Please call me if you have any questions or comments.

_____
(name)

_____
(phone number)

to the biter. Add your phone number to the report so that parents may call you with any questions. If parents indicate that a child is having a repeated problem with biting, supervision should be continued until the problem behavior has ended. (It may be necessary to ask the parent to stay with the child.)

 A parent called recently and said her daughter had come down with chicken pox in the afternoon after attending Sunday School in the morning. What do I need to do?

 Occasionally a child may develop symptoms of a disease later in the day after participating in a class or activity at church. In these cases, it's helpful to send or post a notice to alert parents to the possibility that their children were exposed to the disease. Include possible symptoms and the time period in which children may show symptoms of the disease (see sample below).

Parent Note

We thought you'd want to know!

While in Sunday School at First Church on May 29, your child was exposed to chicken pox.

Symptoms of chicken pox usually include small raised pimples that may have tiny yellow water blisters on top, fever and headache. Symptoms are likely to appear between 11 and 19 days after exposure.

For further information, consult your child's doctor.

Parents and Family

When parents and teachers share similar goals and use similar approaches, teaching God's Word is strengthened. A clearly defined and consistent plan for communicating with parents will develop a strong link between church and home. Long-term positive results in child guidance and spiritual nurture are increased when parents and teachers become partners working together. Conversely, whenever parents are ignored, the impact of any program involving their child is greatly reduced.

Communicating with Parents

Welcome and Information Center:
The easiest way to ensure that you regularly interact with parents is to establish a consistent location at which parents may sign in their children, receive information about their children's classes, register for various children's events, get name tags, etc. Consider the traffic pattern on Sunday mornings and set up a table or counter at a convenient location. (Large churches may need more than one such location.)

Visitors should be able to easily identify the Welcome and Information Center. Post a list of all classes and where they meet and the names and phone numbers of the teachers. Keep available a good supply of current brochures describing your early childhood ministry. The director or leaders of early childhood ministries or a former teacher who is knowledgeable about the programs being offered should be at the location. You may also recruit someone to act as a greeter for 10 to 15 minutes before and after the start of a session but who is then free to attend an adult class or worship service.

Classroom Signs: Outside every class, mount a sign with the name(s) of the teacher(s). Also mount (outside or inside the class) a poster with candid snapshots of teachers in action with students. Add labels with the names of the people pictured and update the photos periodically. Particularly in a larger church in which parents may be unfamiliar with their child's teacher, these signs and photos will help to create a sense of connection.

Handbook or Brochure: Another key method to communicate with parents is to develop a handbook or brochure that describes the programs and procedures of your early childhood ministry. (You may wish to combine this handbook or brochure with the programs for elementary age children.) Update the handbook at least once a year or more frequently if your programs change throughout the year.

Give the handbook to all parents at the beginning of the school year or whenever a family visits your church. Make sure that each teacher also has a copy. Provide copies in the church entryway and make sure that ushers know the location of the books, so they can give them to interested visitors. The handbook should include information on the following topics:

• The goals and purpose of your ministry

• Well-child guidelines for children coming to church

• Greeting and dismissal procedures including your church's plan for child and parent identification

• How you would like parents to provide information about the child (name of child and parents, phone numbers, allergies, etc.)

• Programs available for young children, time schedules (include both starting and ending times), room locations for different ages, facility map, a summary of a typical session plan and description of programs for families and parents of young children

Parent Newsletters: At several significant times throughout the year, it is helpful to send newsletters to parents. (Some churches develop monthly letters.) These newsletters are to help parents understand how they and their children can best benefit from the programs available for families with young children.

The most effective times to send newsletters are at the beginning of the school year, at the start of holiday seasons and at the beginning of summer vacation. Holiday times are natural opportunities to contact parents. Parents are often looking for ways to help their children experience the spiritual significance of such holidays as Christmas and Easter. Some parents just need to be reminded that Sunday School is one of the best ways to help a child discover and enjoy the rich meaning of the holiday. Always include information about something specific that is going on in your early childhood ministry, including the time, place and age groups involved.

Here's What We Did Today

Our Bible story was about

_____

Our Bible verse was

_____

We had fun

_____

We helped each other

_____

"Here's What We Did Today" Forms: Give teachers copies of forms on which they can write brief descriptions of the learning activities in which children participated. For a small class, teachers complete forms for individual children. For larger classes, teachers complete one form before class and photocopy it so that each child has a form to take home. Phrase comments so that they present the purpose of the activity, not just the activity itself. For example, in addition to noting "Our Bible story was about David," add the phrase "who was kind to his friend Jonathan." In addition to writing "We had fun building with blocks," add "and sharing them with my friends Blake and Jorge."

An enlarged copy of the form may be posted at the classroom door so that parents can see at a glance a brief description of their child's activities and be able to talk with the child about the lesson activities. You may also attach by the entrance of each classroom a small white board on which the teacher writes two or three activities in which children participated.

Parent Observation/Open House Days: Periodically invite parents to schedule a Sunday when they will observe a full or partial class session with their child's teacher. Participating in activities with their child will give parents firsthand knowledge of what happens in Sunday School. A small church may schedule all parents to visit on the same day, but a larger church will want to stagger parent visits.

If there are many young families visiting your church or moving into your church's community, offer a facility tour for prospective children and their families. Distribute copies of your handbook. Answer questions about the policies and programs of your early childhood ministry. Provide a brief time with refreshments for teachers and parents to talk together. You may wish to invite a parent whose child has been participating in Sunday School (or another program) to attend the open house or tour. Ask this parent to describe how their family has benefited from the church's early childhood ministry.

Family Support Ideas

The typical Sunday School teacher tends to feel that the effort of preparing lessons and guiding sessions is more than enough responsibility. But when Sunday School teachers work in isolation from the child's family, they cannot be aware of individual circumstances. Help your teachers understand that developing an interest in their children's families is not adding a new task to their teaching ministry. Rather, it is enriching their ministry, providing greater satisfaction in teaching.

Class Rosters: A basic step in helping your teachers know the families of their students is to provide teachers with up-to-date rosters that list each child's name, address, phone number, birthday and first and last names of parents and siblings. Rosters can be compiled from registration cards (see sample on p. 64) and may need to be updated several times throughout the year. Displaying rosters (including pictures, if possible) at each classroom door makes it easy for parents and children to find their classrooms and feel welcome.

It is especially helpful if rosters not only list the names of children actively involved in Sunday School (or another program), but also list the names of children from church families who are not actively involved. Encourage teachers to periodically make contact with these children and families to give a personal invitation to attend class. Suggest that teachers use lists to make contacts informally (in the church parking lot, at an adult event, in the grocery store, at the mall, at the park, etc.).

Follow-Up Suggestions: While the goal of communicating by card or phone call with each child during the week would be overwhelming, encourage your teachers to set a goal of communicating with at least one child and/his or her family each week. This smaller task can be accomplished easily if teachers have been provided with class rosters, note cards, stickers to enclose with brief notes, stamps, etc. Enclose all the items in a resealable bag, along with a pen.

Pay special attention to the ways in which visitors are contacted in the week or two after their first visit. In addition to mailing personalized "thanks for visiting" cards or letters, some churches give each visiting child a gift bag with several inexpensive play items (stickers, crayons, stamps, etc.) as well as printed information about your church.

Creative Support Ideas: Keep an ongoing list of special ways in which the church can support families.

• Plan a series of parent education classes that give parents advice and guidelines for common parenting issues. Invite a speaker (a knowledgeable person in your church or community) to address an issue of interest to parents—discipline, activities to do at home, holiday celebration ideas, safety in the home, how to use take-home papers effectively, etc. Include a time for parents to talk together and trade ideas and thoughts about the challenges of child rearing. Offering six to eight sessions over a period of several months will encourage participation by parents whose time is limited.

• One to three times a year plan PTO (parent-teacher organization) meetings at which information about teaching children spiritual truths is presented. Use the information presented in "How Young Children Learn" (see pp. 7-8) as the basis for this meeting.

• Send out copies of articles of special interest to parents (available from Christian parenting magazines).

• Plan ways the church can support a family when a new baby is born or when a child or parent is ill (meals, transportation, child care, etc.).

• Develop a prayer-partner system in which members of the church family are linked with parents of young children. Prayer partners can share requests by phone, e-mail or personal meetings.

• Establish a shelf, table or corner near the early childhood classrooms where books and magazines of interest to parents of young children can be displayed. Stock this useful library with books about child rearing, activities to enjoy with young children, age-level characteristics, etc. Encourage parents to sign out these books, returning them in a week or two. Invite parents whose children have grown beyond the preschool stage to donate books or videos they found helpful as parents of young children.

• Give visiting families a welcome pack that includes information about church programs, stickers for children to play with, registration cards, letter from a parent describing the benefits of participating in church programs, refrigerator magnet with church information, etc.

• Connect grandparents to young families by forming a Grandparents' Club. Invite senior adults who do not have grandchildren or whose grandchildren do not live nearby to join in informal meetings with young families—particularly those whose parents are no longer living or who do not live nearby.

• Once a month offer free baby-sitting to parents of young children during the dinner hour. Parents can eat at home or at a restaurant, enjoying a special time of "adults only" conversation. Include these guidelines: (1) parents reserve space a week ahead of time; (2) when checking in their children, parents leave a phone number where they can be reached and sign a permission slip.

Questions and Answers

  The parents of two children in our Sunday School seem to regularly complain about the care their children receive. What is the best way to respond to these parents?

When talking to a parent who has a complaint, listen closely to what the parent is saying. Ask questions to make sure you have all the needed information to respond to the complaint. If a problem has occurred due to an oversight or mistake, apologize and thank the parent for bringing the matter to your attention.

If the complaint is related to an ongoing situation, invite the parent to suggest specific actions that would remedy the existing problem. Let the parent know you will do your best to resolve the situation. Follow up the complaint by letting the parent know what changes have been made, if possible.

If the complaint is not really valid, thank the parent for voicing concern, but point out why the class or program operates as it does.

 Occasionally a parent will want to have both of his or her children in the same Sunday School class, usually because one of the children becomes upset at being separated from the other. Should we let the children attend the same class?

 This situation is most likely to occur when a new family begins attending your church. It is best to address the situation at the beginning. "We're glad to have Marah and Micah attend the same class for one or two weeks while they get used to our church. But after several weeks, Marah will probably be bored in Micah's class. Then it will be time to move her into her own class, so she can enjoy the activities of children who are the same age as she is."

Teacher Training Articles

This section contains dozens of concise informative articles dealing with issues of concern to teachers of young children.

Use these articles in both preventive and prescriptive form: for staff training before problems occur, and as a remedy to problem situations already in place.

Photocopy the articles of your choice and distribute, or use selected topics as the basis for teacher training sessions. Either way, it's a ready-made resource at your fingertips!

Activity Pages: More Than a Time-Filler!

Purpose

Some days, a class of overexcited, rowdy preschoolers can tempt us to plunk down an activity page in front of each one and gratefully take a break. But this resource has great potential for learning if we stay actively involved!

The student activity page has a twofold purpose: first, to provide each child with a personalized visual aid to use in reviewing the Bible story; second, to help children think and talk about what the Bible truth means in their daily lives. Not a craft or an art activity, it is an interactive way to reinforce that day's Bible truth.

Plan

Every Quarter

At the beginning of the quarter, separate and store each lesson's pages and stickers in a labeled envelope or clear resealable bag. (A paper cutter can make cutting pages and sticker strips easier.) Many churches have senior citizens or older children involved with weekday club programs who can do an excellent job of preparing activity page materials.

Every Week

Before each class, take out that lesson's page and a set of stickers. Become familiar with how the page works. Prepare children's pages if needed by prefolding and then unfolding. When a page requires cutting, depending on the skill level of your class, precut some or all of the cuts.

During class before handing out the pages, talk with the children about the pictures on the page, so they understand its purpose. Use your page and stickers to demonstrate how to complete the page (cutting, folding, etc.). Seeing your demonstration will provide a visual guide for children.

During this demonstration and while children complete their own pages, provide opportunities for children to talk about the scene or action on the page. Ask simple specific questions to help children recall the action the page illustrates. For example, begin the story and then ask, "What happened next?" Let a volunteer tell. Involve as many children as possible. In classes where children are just beginning to use words to communicate, suggest a child answer your question by pointing to the appropriate figure on the activity page.

Participation Tips

Repetition and Review

Young children enjoy the color, the stickers and the action of the activity pages. More than that, young children learn best through repetition! The activity page provides a fresh way to illustrate and repeat the Bible story, both in class and then at home with family. And with hands and minds busy, children often respond freely and listen eagerly as you guide the conversation. Be sure to use the questions and comments provided in your curriculum to help children think about and talk about the page.

Assistance

Try to assist only when a child cannot complete a task. As you get to know the children in your class, you will know which children may need extra help.

If an older child is not interested in doing the activity page, say, "It's OK if you don't want to work on your page right now. But

all of us need to sit at the table together." Often, after a few moments, the child will decide that the page is an acceptable activity after all! You may also provide a quiet alternate task, such as drawing on blank paper or looking at books. Send the uncompleted activity page home and suggest that parents may invite the child to work on the page when interest is shown.

Some children may make a few marks on the page and announce, "I'm done." While children should never be forced to complete an activity, there are often questions that can be asked to encourage further participation. "Everyone gets to color the flowers a different color. What color are you going to choose?" "Which picture on your page shows the beginning of the story? The end?" Engage the child about the scene or action on the page or invite him or her to retell the Bible story.

Folding and Cutting

To help a child fold his or her own page, hold the page in the proper position. Then tell the child to press and rub where he or she wants the fold.

When a child does his or her own cutting, hold the page taut for him or her.

Stickers, Taping and Gluing

For very young children, peel the backing from around a set of stickers to make them easy for small fingers to remove.

To simplify tape use, pull off and stick pieces of tape on the edge of the table, rather than handing a child a roll of tape.

Some lessons suggest optional touch-and-feel materials to add to the activity page. Gluing is done most easily with glue sticks. However, small glue bottles also work well if you tell children to use tiny dots of glue. Try seeing who can make the smallest dots!

Art Center: Creative Art for Young Children

Art activities are among the most used—and most misunderstood—experiences offered to young children. Young children have no sense whatsoever of what adults expect them to produce when art materials are offered. They are small scientists: for them, art materials are not a means to make a pretty product by adult standards but the means to discover what happens when, for instance, random paper scraps are stacked together and glued into a pile!

Process, Not Product

For young children, using art materials is about the experience of creating and the process of discovering. Remember that for young children it is the *process*, not the *product*, that matters. Encourage children to explore materials freely. Relax and recognize that sometimes it is a greater learning experience to swirl the glue with fingers than it is to create what the teacher had in mind! Art gives children the chance to express their feelings and thoughts and to release tension as well. Give them freedom to experiment creatively.

Helping, Not Hindering

As a child and teacher use art materials together in a relaxed and creative way, natural opportunities arise for conversation. Such teachable moments often provide the perfect times to help a child understand vital Bible truths! "I see lots of blue in your picture, James. What other things did God make that are blue?" "God gave you hands that can draw lots of little circles, Josie. Let's thank Him!" Include God in your conversation through word, prayer or song to positively reinforce how much God values that child!

As children work, relate the Bible verse to what you see children doing. "Lee, I see you gave Michael a turn with the blue crayon. Thank you. Our Bible says to share with other people. You are doing what God's Word says to do!" "Lena, Weston doesn't have enough room. What could you do to help him? Thank you for moving over, Lena. You are being kind. God's Word tells us to be kind."

When a child shows you his or her work, invite the child into conversation about the art. NEVER ask, "What is it?" The comment to make is, "Emily, tell me about your picture!" or "I see many squiggly lines, Kyle—tell me about those lines." And NEVER attempt to fix or finish what you think needs to be changed in any child's art.

If a child says, "Draw it for me," suggest, "Let's see how much you can do by yourself first." Encourage the child and help him or her feel assured that no one will judge his or her work.

A child may comment, "Leo's picture is ugly!" or "He copied me. That's not fair!" Deal gently with both the critic and the criticized. "Mason, Leo made his picture the way he wanted it." You may also say, "If Leo's picture is like your picture, that's OK. Leo must have really liked your picture." Don't put down the child who voiced the criticism; instead, help the child see that each person's work is valued.

Basic Materials

Make sure you have plenty of the following supplies on hand: newspaper or plastic tablecloths (to protect surfaces), scissors, glue bottles and glue sticks, markers, crayons, chalk, tape, play dough, discarded magazines and catalogs, collage materials (yarn, ribbon, cotton balls, chenille wire), colored and white construction paper, stapler and staples, paint smocks (old men's short-sleeved shirts from a thrift shop serve well) and butcher paper.

Preparation

For children to enjoy an art project, they need to hear as few warnings as possible. They need to feel successful. As you get to know the personalities and capabilities of each child, you can tailor the activity to the group's needs. And a little preparation will go a long way in keeping a small mess from becoming a big one!

Cover tabletops and floors with newspaper or plastic tablecloths. Secure on all sides with masking tape.

Keep a supply of premoistened towelettes, no-rinse hand-wiping solution or paper towels handy for messy fingers and small spills. Set a trash can where children can clean up easily.

Activities that use potentially messy materials (glue, paint, etc.) may be difficult if your teacher/child ratio is too large or if you do not have adequate space or furniture. In such cases, you may need to substitute easier materials (crayons, etc.) to deal with.

Bible: Teaching God's Word to Young Children

It doesn't seem logical that a book completed nearly 2,000 years ago would have much to say to young children. But the Bible is far more than an ancient classic. The Word of God is living and active. It applies to every life in every age! For those of us who teach young children, however, it's up to us to help make the words and ideas of an ancient book something that relates to a young child's world.

The Bible is listed as a material in every activity for a very good reason: although you can easily quote Bible verses, children need to associate the words with the Bible. This way they will know that the Bible is the source of these words. Frequently emphasize that the stories in the Bible are true.

The most direct use of and application of the Bible will come during conversation as natural opportunities arise. With your Bible open to the day's memory verse, say the verse aloud. Children will naturally associate using the Bible as a source of information and guidance in everyday situations. Because young children are "here and now" people, they need to have you see and interpret their actions in light of what the Bible says. Young children have a limited grasp of ideas; this kind of natural, direct Bible teaching helps them know what Bible ideas can look like, sound like and act like.

Consider keeping a large-print Bible in your classroom. Display it prominently and use sticky notes or colorful bookmarks to help children find Bible verses. You'll find children enjoy pretending to read (or reading) the words you have marked.

While some older preschoolers may memorize Bible verses easily (especially when the words are sung to familiar music), don't pressure all young children to memorize the Bible verses. Make your main goal to help children understand the content of what God is saying to us and how we can obey Him.

Bible Learning Activities: Using Bible Learning Activities Effectively

As Christians, we have far more to teach children than facts and words. It's not enough for a child to hear us read from the Bible or even for a child to memorize it. Words alone are the least effective way humans learn! When we hear words only, we must build a mental image based on previous information. Because a child's knowledge and experience is so limited, he or she is not likely to gain a real understanding through hearing words alone.

For an idea to make any sense to a young child, he or she must DO something with it. And the word that describes most of what a young child does is "play." However, a young child is not yet able to play with *ideas*. So a child must build understanding through playing with something he or she *can touch*. That's the reason for hands-on activity. First-hand activity (or play) is a young child's most effective way to learn! Young children can learn Bible truth effectively through active play experiences. As a child draws, plays a game, builds with blocks or holds a doll, natural opportunities arise for the teacher to link the child's actions to what God's Word says. When we describe the ways children are putting God's Word into action, we turn play into Bible learning. Play then takes on a greater purpose!

For instance, during a simple beanbag toss game we can comment, "Ainsley, you gave Josh a turn to toss the beanbag. Thank you! That is a way to be kind. Our Bible tells us to be kind." As we effectively link a Bible truth to Ainsley's actions, she now has a concrete example of a way to be kind!

Providing repeated opportunities to think and talk about Bible truths creates more and more of those mental building blocks. As you participate with children in an activity, it's important to watch for opportunities to acknowledge and encourage children you see acting in ways that you can relate to the Bible truth.

A Bible learning activity is different from a craft. Crafts, while offering enjoyable experiences to children, are usually limited in the amount of Bible learning that can occur because the focus is usually more on following directions than on the total process that the child experiences. A meaningful session for young children should provide more Bible learning activities than crafts. The chart on page 92 will help you distinguish whether an activity is a craft or a Bible learning activity. (Obviously, most Bible learning activities that involve art will have some characteristics of crafts, and some craft projects can be guided in ways that engage children in active Bible learning.)

Busy Hands Mean Open Minds

When children are fully involved in an activity they enjoy, we have the privilege of seeing them simply being themselves. When we observe them, we understand more about how they think. Also, children whose hands are busy are often eager to talk. Ask open-ended what-do-you-think questions. Avoid questions that have one-word answers. This chance to listen helps us determine what a child does or does not understand. Then we are able to respond in ways that truly meet that child's needs!

Watch for moments when a child experiences curiosity, expectation or frustration. In that moment of heightened interest, a child is most receptive to a new idea or the security of a familiar truth. Remember the words "acknowledge" and "encourage" as your conversational cornerstones. For example, when Kim's block tower is finished, he looks around with satisfaction. He's eager to know you see him and share his joy. "I see you finished your tower, Kim. It looks very strong. God has given you good hands and a good mind. You're a good builder!"

Choice Creates Interest

Children are usually more content to stay with an activity they have chosen, rather than one they have been assigned. When you provide several learning activities (each led by a teacher) that appeal to different learning styles and interests, discipline problems often diminish and children enjoy finishing what they began. The child who is absorbed in an activity he or she has chosen is in a prime position for learning!

Some children find it difficult to begin an activity when they first arrive. They need help in learning to choose. Allow the child to move at his or her own pace. "Liam, when you're ready, you may build with blocks in the corner with Mr. Sanchez or glue these pictures with me. Watch for a while if you like."

When we provide a choice of several activities, we should not expect young children to stay focused on one activity for more than a few minutes. The younger the child, the shorter the attention span; again, this is part of helping a child learn. When the child moves back and forth between activities, remain quietly observant for ways you can connect his or her activity to the Bible truth being taught.

A child needs to use every sense—tasting, touching, smelling, hearing and seeing—to learn effectively. This is why it's important to provide activity choices that may not appeal to you personally. When we give children activity choices that involve as many senses and learning styles as possible, we send them the message that we want them to choose, learn and enjoy! It's another way to show the loving acceptance Jesus modeled.

Bible Learning Activity or Craft?

Bible Learning Activity	Craft
• Children explore, create and discover with the provided materials.	• Children follow predetermined pattern.
• Teacher talks informally with children, asking questions and guiding the conversation toward the Bible learning aims; children talk with each other as well as with the teacher.	• Teacher gives instructions with little opportunity for children to talk.
• Focus is on the process (including the use of materials), group interaction and the connection to the Bible truth.	• Focus is on the product.
• Children choose from two or more activities and choose how they want to complete the activity.	• Only one project is offered and children are expected to produce a similar result.
• Small groups work with one activity at a time and move freely from one activity to the other.	• Children all work on the same project at the same time.

Blocks Center: More Than Play!

If there is a spot in an early childhood classroom that is a perpetual favorite with some children, it is the block area! When young children play with blocks, they experiment with the physical properties of solid objects. They solve engineering problems, learn to make decisions and practice cooperation and sharing. Blocks also provide a place for children to have the physical release of large-muscle movement and the freedom of imaginative play. Never dismiss the block area as unimportant!

Block-Play Stages

Young children go through very distinctive stages of block play.

Stage One: Blocks are carried and put into or taken from containers.

Stage Two: Blocks are stacked, built into small piles or laid next to each other. (Twos and threes are often working side by side at this point in parallel play.)

Stage Three: A space is enclosed and bridged. (This is an important step in developing problem-solving skills.)

Stage Four: Patterns of blocks are arranged to make a structure. These patterns are often symmetrical and sometimes built with others.

Stage Five: Structures that are built are named and used for dramatic play in the block area.

Stage Six: A construction is cooperatively planned and built with others ("Let's make

an airport!"); the structure is named before it is built, and other items are used to enhance the imaginary play.

By the time children are four or five years old, they have usually moved into the last stages of block-play development. However, some children will use block play area as a place to relax through using the large-muscle activity or the chance to work alone. There is no right or wrong way to play with blocks as long as they are being used safely.

Teacher's Role

Just because children are absorbed and busy in block play does not mean it is time to take a break! Instead, look for ways to help children enrich their play, resolve conflicts or think through situations. "Here is a little horse. Would you like to put it in your barn, Joycelyn?" "Karen, you and Mandy both want the same block. What is a way you can solve your problem?" "Kevin, is your road as long as your arm? How could you find out?"

Sometimes children will begin to build items of their own choosing (airports, towers, roads, houses, etc.), even when you have stated "Today we're going to build a big block boat and talk about a time Jesus traveled on a boat." It's OK for children to build their own structures. However, it is important that you stay involved with the block building. Look for ways you can connect the child's activity with the Bible story or verse. "Bradley, you're building an airplane. When have you been on an airplane? When Jesus lived on Earth, there were no airplanes. One day Jesus traveled on a boat."

Don't intervene every minute, but when you see frustration surfacing, ask a question that will help a child recognize the next step in solving the problem. "What do you think will help your tower stand up better? How can you make the bottom of your building wider, Jayce?" If a block becomes a weapon, simply repeat the rule: "Blocks are only for building. What would you like to build now, Zach? We could build a zoo."

This is also prime time to relate children's actions to the Bible truth. Conversation with young builders can give them *mental* building blocks of ways to know and do what God's Word says. "You built a bridge, Ron! I also saw you give Joe a turn with the long blocks you were using. You shared with Joe. Thank you. Our Bible verse tells us to do good and share." Block building provides firsthand experiences in practicing concepts such as sharing, helping, taking turns and exercising self-control.

Basic Materials

Provide many different sizes, shapes and colors of wooden, cardboard or plastic blocks. Blocks for children under three years of age should be lightweight and easy to manipulate. Provide enough blocks so that several children can build at the same time. Four- and five-year-olds need a larger number and variety of blocks. Wooden unit blocks are the preferred basic set. (Note: In a set of unit blocks, each block is a unit of a larger block; two of the smallest blocks equal one of the larger size, etc.)

Sturdy toy cars and trucks should be a part of every block area. Other accessory toys include toy people, toy animals and toy trees. Four- and five-year-olds enjoy using signs (traffic signs, building signs, etc.) in their block play. Even simple recyclable items like clean oatmeal boxes and film canisters provide children with materials to expand their creativity. Manipulative building toys, such as Legos or Lincoln Logs, integrate easily into block play.

Block Storage

Blocks and accessory toys should be stored on low open shelves to make it easy for children to see and help themselves. Avoid piling blocks into bins if possible. Instead, trace around each block shape onto colorful contact paper. Attach the shape on the front of the shelf where that shape of block belongs. The sorting and matching needed to put away blocks in their places becomes a learning process in itself. If you have no shelves, gather some sturdy cardboard boxes, fold flaps inside and lay boxes on their sides for shelves.

To keep a space for children to move back and forth to the block shelves, lay a masking-tape line several feet away from the fronts of the shelves. Tell children to always build on the other side of this line, so others have room to remove and return blocks without knocking down anyone else's work.

Providing adequate space and high-quality blocks is a valuable gift to your children! Young builders can know and do what God's Word says.

Block Rules

Only a few clear rules need to apply in the block area:

• Stack blocks no higher than your chin.

• Keep blocks in the block area.

• Use blocks only for building.

• Knock down only your own towers and only when no one is in the way.

Books: Tips for Reading with Young Children

In a world awhirl with in-your-face nonstop entertainment, stories well read or engagingly told give children a place to use their own imaginations. It provides a relaxed time and a quiet activity for them to enjoy. More than that, it provides the impetus for a lifelong love of reading, which helps greatly in guiding children to want to read the Bible for themselves. Children of every age love a good story!

Provide a comfortable place for children to look at books. Several carpet squares or comfortable pillows and a few books (related to the aims of the lesson you are teaching) are all that is needed. Invite children to look at books during Bible learning activities or when children finish an activity early. If a bookshelf is needed, provide one made with angled shelves that make it easy to organize and display books.

Books for Preschoolers

Expect that many children may be more interested in the pictures of a book than the story itself. Always be sure that any book for young children is appropriately illustrated. Some illustrations may be beautiful; but if they are not clear to a child, they will be meaningless, and children will soon lose interest. Remember that as you are reading the words in a book, children are viewing the pictures. The illustrations must relate directly to the words. Pace your words so that children can both look at each picture and hear the words you are reading.

Select books that don't have too many words on each page. If it takes too long to read the words, children will not be able to stay focused on the story action. When a book has too much text on the page, simply talk about the picture or summarize the content. Don't expect children to guess what is going on in a picture that is not clear or not related to the words you are saying.

Stories for two- and three-year-olds should be about familiar subjects (animals, babies, families, etc.) and about family activities (playing, helping, eating, sleeping, etc.). Fours and fives enjoy stories and pictures about family, home and friends; but they are also interested in stories about nature and machines. Simple stories about Jesus should be included for all ages.

While a measure of fantasy or pretending is valuable for young children, be cautious at church about using books with talking animals or plants or imaginary creatures. One of our major objectives at church is to communicate the truth of Bible stories. If one minute we are reading about cartoon characters and the next minute we talk about Jesus, we create confusion for the children.

For greater involvement, use books that are predictable or have repeating phrases. When words or phrases are repeated throughout the book, children anticipate them and will say the repeating words with you as you read. This repetition further involves them in the story. Of course, they will likely be interested in reading the same book over and over again!

Tips for Reading with Several Children

Arrange books in a quiet area of the room. A child may browse through a book alone or join others to listen to a story. Remain nearby to read the text or talk about the pictures; otherwise, a child may become bored in a few seconds.

Sit on the floor or at a low table. Interest children in the book or teaching pictures

by looking at them yourself. Make comments aloud. "Look at all these big animals!" Soon children will come to see what you are doing.

As you turn the pages of a book, ask simple questions to help children "see" picture details. Also ask open-ended questions. "Where do you think this boy and his dad are going?" You can also help build a child's vocabulary by repeating the child's reply in a complete sentence and by occasionally adding a word. "Alexis, what is this? You are right! It's a bird. It's a red bird. God made the birds."

Tips for Reading Aloud

One of the greatest complaints of children is "I can't SEE!" When reading a book to a group, be sure the illustrations are large and clear enough to be seen by every child. When you first turn to a new page, hold the book out for each child to get a good look before you proceed.

If you cannot sit on the floor, sit on a low chair. The book should be held a little higher than children's eye level.

Hold the book to one side facing it toward the children as much as possible. This helps you maintain eye contact and gives children a chance to see the pictures in the book as well as the expressions on your face (the more expressive your face, the better!).

• Use an expressive voice; change voices for different characters if you can. Becoming familiar with the story ahead of time will help you plan for character voices.

• If you read a favorite story repeatedly, put together a prop box for that story. Include items mentioned in the story or several puppets. When the story is read, invite children to take turns holding up the items or moving the puppets at the appropriate times.

Characteristics: Developmental Milestones of Twos, Threes, Fours and Fives

"Aren't all three-year-olds alike?" The answer to that question is both yes and no! Every child develops in a unique way. At any given chronological age, children's developmental differences will vary greatly. But some basic developmental guidelines can help you become both a better observer and a more effective helper.

Twos

Physical: Twos are able to walk, climb, scribble on paper, build block towers, fill a container with small objects and turn pages in a book. Although large muscles are fairly well developed, twos often stumble and fall. They move all the time! Small muscles are not yet well developed. Twos are often in the process of being potty trained. They enjoy simple songs with movement and large-muscle activities and need room to roam as well as quiet time activities.

Mental and Emotional: Twos have a short attention span, and they learn best through using all their senses. A two is often eager to do things without help and uses "no" frequently as a way to define his or her separate identity. Twos may say many words and some simple sentences and recognize their names in print. Twos enjoy retelling a story or activity, which increases their sense of mastery.

Social: Twos have very little concept about other people's rights or feelings. "MINE!" is a favorite word. Using distraction and redirection works far better than reasoning when there are disputes. Twos play mainly by themselves or play next to but not with other children. Get on their eye level. Talk about what you see them doing to help them know you notice them and love them.

Spiritual: Twos can learn that God made everything, that God cares about them, that Jesus is God's special Son, that the Bible is God's special book and that Jesus and Bible stories are true. Talk and sing about God often.

Threes

Physical: Threes have increased small-muscle ability, can unlace and remove shoes and button and unbutton clothing, draw pictures and name the people and items which they draw. They build more complicated block structures and are usually completely potty trained. Threes enjoy stringing big beads, putting together simple puzzles and playing with dough, as well as singing songs and hearing simple stories. They may begin to use scissors.

Mental and Emotional: Threes may be able to write part of their names and can usually identify colors and repeat simple rhymes and songs. Threes begin to imitate and pretend. They can wait for short periods of time and may show more sympathy for others.

Social: Threes may interact with other children more as they play, although sharing and taking turns are still not habitual. Give good eye contact at eye level and be sure to show you see, hear and love them.

Spiritual: Threes can understand that Jesus was born as a baby and grew up to do kind things, that God is good and that Jesus loves us. Threes understand more about God's love and nature through loving actions than through spoken words.

Fours

Physical: Fours begin a period of rapid growth. Coordination catches up in both small and large muscles. They still need a great deal of space and time to explore and enjoy the creative process.

Mental and Emotional: Fours begin to ask why and how. Their attention spans are still short, but they can concentrate for longer periods. Fours may often test the limits of what is acceptable behavior.

Social: Fours begin to enjoy being with other children in group activities. They want to please adults and usually love their teachers. Give each child a chance to feel successful by helping in some way. Provide ways they can sing, pray and talk together.

Spiritual: Fours begin to understand more about Jesus: that He is God's Son, that He lived on Earth to show God's love for us, that He died but rose again and is still alive. Fours can also be taught that the Bible tells us ways to obey God and that we can talk to God in prayer.

Fives

Physical: Fives are learning to tie their own shoes, to cut with scissors successfully and to draw pictures that are recognizable to others. Girls move ahead of boys in development. Coordination has usually become excellent.

Mental and Emotional: Fives are often able to write their own names, copy words and letters and may even read some words. Fives can talk accurately about recent events and speak understandably. They love to learn why, still seek adult approval and love to discover for themselves through play and experimenting. Encourage them to think by asking what-could-happen-next and how-could-you-solve-this open-ended questions.

Social: Fives enjoy extended periods of cooperative play, usually with one or two others. They enjoy group activities and need to feel that they are seen and heard. Need for attention may cause them to act in negative ways. Give attention before negative actions occur. Give good eye contact at eye level and be sure to show you see, hear and love them.

Spiritual: Fives are the most likely to respond by talking about the Bible story or Bible verse, and some children will understand that being kind as Jesus was is something they can do. Some children, especially those from Christian homes, may be interested in becoming members of God's family. Help them feel confident that God hears their prayers and that God wants to help them. As with all young children, they think literally and concretely and cannot understand abstract ideas like "Jesus in my heart" or "born again."

The most important way we teach young children about God's love is to show them! As we get on their level, listen to them, encourage them and make them feel secure, they begin to link God's love with the joy, excitement and security they feel from you.

Choices: Helping Children Make Good Choices

When the adult makes all the choices (what color paper to use in an art activity, where each person sits at the table, what game to play, etc.), the adult is also the one doing the most learning. In order for children to truly be learning, they must be more than passive receivers of information. Giving children repeated opportunities to make choices provides many benefits, not only to the child, but also to the adult.

The Benefits of Making Choices

Making choices helps a child develop a sense of independence. This is not independence from authority and direction but independence that produces responsibility, allowing the child to make good choices. Never allowing a child to make a choice can be harmful, now and in the years to come. If a child is always looking for someone else to make decisions, he or she can become a pawn for a strong authority figure to lead astray.

Making small choices, such as which color crayon to use or whether to build with blocks or play with the dress-up clothes, can actually help prepare a young child to make life's larger decisions. Because the child eventually must "choose . . . this day whom you will serve" (Joshua 24:15), we must help children develop wise choice-making skills. The child who is rarely allowed to make decisions may find it harder to make the ultimate decision of responding to Jesus Christ.

A child develops a sense of responsibility through making choices. A responsible person is one who makes a choice after having fully considered the consequences of that choice. Learning to be accountable for choices made will help the child in making responsible choices.

Allowing children to make some of their own choices will help you avoid discipline problems. Children's behaviors are more positive when they are doing something they have chosen. In contrast, when a child is told to do something he or she doesn't want to do, he or she becomes unhappy and usually will let everyone know it.

Allowing a child to make choices tells the child you believe he or she is capable of making a decision. Your trust is an essential foundation for a child's healthy development.

How to Present Choices

Limit the number of choices to two or three, and be firm about behavior that is not an acceptable option. "Would you rather build with the blocks or glue pictures? It is not time yet to play outside."

Offer choices that are not mutually exclusive. "Which book would you rather look at first? The book about friends or the one about animals?"

Comment positively about the different choices children make. "Abby chose yellow paper for her collage and Andrew chose black. Each of us can choose a different color."

Christmas: What's the Main Idea?

Christmas! The word itself stirs feelings of extraordinary excitement. And rightly so. During the holiday season there are reminders of the season everywhere. But let's be sure our children know what the excitement is really about.

How can we help a young child realize that Christmas is a celebration of gratitude to God for His wonderful gift of love? There are several ways you can make the biblical and spiritual aspects of Christmas meaningful and attractive to a young child.

Help children know the simple facts of Jesus' birth as they are recorded in Scripture.

• Tell or read the story of the first Christmas to children from Bible storybooks or from an easy-to-understand version of the Bible.

• Allow children to participate in assembling a manger scene. Retell the story of Jesus' birth as they move the figures, or invite children to tell the story as you move the figures.

Help children feel that Jesus is God's best gift of love.

• Remember that much of a child's response is a reflection of the attitudes he or she sees from you. Nurture feelings of joy, love and thankfulness in your child.

• In the presence of your child, give thanks to God for Jesus.

• Include children in your church's plans for expressing love to Jesus by caring and loving others (collect canned foods or personal care items for a rescue mission, fill a shoebox with age-appropriate gifts to be given to needy children, etc.). With your child, talk about the gifts the wise men gave to Jesus to show their love for Him. Explain that we give gifts to others at Christmas to show our love for them.

Help your child express joy, excitement and feelings of love.

• Show gladness as you sing about Jesus' birth.

• Be sensitive to moments when it is natural to talk about Jesus' birth and encourage your child to thank God in prayer for sending Jesus to be born.

Keep Santa in the proper perspective.

• Avoid referring to Santa as a real person. If a child talks about Santa, say "Talking about Santa is fun. But it's even better to talk about Jesus who loves us all year long."

• Avoid the "What do you want Santa to bring you for Christmas?" and "Be good for Santa" emphases.

• Keep the meaning of Christmas clear by frequently commenting on it. "Christmas is a happy time because it is Jesus' birthday. People give presents to show their love. God showed His love by giving us Jesus."

100

Circle Time: Tips for Leading Children in a Large Group

When we consider that many children now watch 35 to 40 hours per week of visual media (TV, videos, computer games), it's easy to wonder if a simple group time can keep a child's interest. Thankfully, the answer is yes! When all children in the classroom sing together, play a game together or listen to a story together, the live interaction is better than any interactive media experience. It's also a powerful place to demonstrate the love of God and connect His Word to children's daily lives!

Be Prepared

Because these large-group experiences can have great value, use a few preparation strategies to maximize the time. Nothing loses the interest of a group of children faster than a teacher rummaging around, trying to find or prepare something!

Before the class session, place the materials you will need for group time at the group-time area. If you are able to store items in your room from week to week, consider keeping a small rolling cart of stackable bins or baskets to hold group-time materials: flannel figures, story items, puppets and nature objects can all be organized neatly, ready for use. If you choose to have large-group time in a different area, your materials are portable. And children are usually fascinated to see what will come out of the baskets next!

During the class session, while one teacher is leading the large group, the other teachers and helpers in the room sit among the children. These teachers and helpers are then able to model appropriate behavior as well as be available to redirect the attention of a wandering child.

Be Flexible

Limit the total number of children in your classroom to 20 to 24 children. Keeping the group this size allows for children to see the visuals easily and gives each child opportunity to interact with you and others in the group. Some churches prefer to have even smaller groups for Bible story time so that personal attention is given to each child.

Consider the length of the activities or story and customize the length of any activity to meet the needs of your group. Keep in mind that the length of a Bible story should be approximately one minute for each year of the child's age. If an activity is working well, be prepared to expand it! If an activity is not working, have other activities ready as alternatives. Always be alert for that restless inattention that tells you it is time to change activities. If you are working with other helpers, the helper may provide another quiet activity for a child who is too young or too restless to stay with the group.

Be Inviting

Set a tone for group time that will make children eager to participate! As soon as one or two children are ready, begin with a fun interactive activity that will draw children into group time. Sing a song in which children's names are sung or spoken as they arrive to help even the most reluctant one get to the circle before the song is over, so he or she can be recognized. Instead of a song, you may play a game that allows each child to participate. When you begin group time with a song or an activity that looks and sounds like fun, each child feels welcomed and important.

Be Visible

If there's one consistent complaint voiced during a group time, it's "I can't SEE!" Instead of seating children in a semicircle, try staggering carpet squares or other markers in two or three theater-style rows, so each child has a clear view of you and the visuals you use.

Hold a visual aid up next to your face or set it on a nearby low chair so that you can maintain good eye contact and so that children can see your expressions as they hear you tell the story. If children's attention wanders, put the visual facedown in your lap and say, "I'm going to show this picture when you are looking quietly at me."

The younger the children are who you teach, the more likely it will be that they will want to get up and handle the visual aids. Gently redirect them to a sitting position. "As soon as you sit on the floor, I'll show each one of you the picture." Then show the picture to each individual child.

Be Observant

It's easy for one child's inattention to completely distract the whole group and the teacher besides! If you observe that a child is having difficulty keeping his or her attention focused during the group activities, try one of these options:

• Invite the child by name to participate in some way. "Jon, can you hold up your hands like the man in the story did?"

• Begin a song or finger fun to refocus everyone's attention.

• Thank children who are participating and paying attention. "Teresa, thank you for watching me while I told the story."

Cleanup: Cleaning Up for Fun!

Taking care of materials and equipment is a basic part of life learning. When you have a positive attitude toward cleanup, you can make it interesting, giving clear expectations and generous encouragement and appreciation. When children enter a room that is reasonably neat and clean, children are more likely to respond to your guidance in keeping the room neat. Point out how there is room to play a game when the toys are put away, or comment on how everyone can easily find something to build with when the blocks are stacked on shelves. Take delight in pointing out the ways children are helping, showing love and obeying!

Cleaning Up Takes Time

Be sure to give cleaning up enough time. It should not be an afterthought. Plan this time into your schedule to help children understand that cleaning up is a valuable activity. Five to ten minutes before cleanup time, move to each activity area to give the children advance notice. "We'll be cleaning up soon."

When children are not ready to transition into cleaning up, let them work a little longer and tell them it is fine to do so. But if they have no choice, be clear! Don't ask, "Would you like to clean up?" Say, "It's time to clean up now. We need to put away the blocks. The puzzles need to go back into the racks." If a child has a hard time making the transition, acknowledge his or her feelings. "I see you were having a lot of fun. It's time to put the puzzles away now. But we'll be sure to put them out again the next time we are together." (Be sure to keep your word!)

Remember that to most young children the concept of cleaning up may not be any more clear than the concept of paying bills or flying to Atlanta. They may have some experience of it but not much genuine understanding! They need the tasks broken into manageable portions. Directions need to tell them what they can do, not what to avoid. Instead of saying, "Don't start playing with the blocks again!" try, "Liam, you and Sean need to finish putting the blocks on the shelves. Would you like to stack the long blocks first or the short blocks?"

- Give plenty of advance notice.
- Make your expectations clear.
- State your directions positively.
- Give a choice to refocus resistant helpers.

Cleaning Up Can Be Fun

Make cleaning up an interesting experience and a way to have some fun!

Games

- Play I Spy. As children clean up, simply say, "I spy something orange on the floor." The challenge is to spot and put away the item you described. Acknowledge the child who puts away the item. "Robert, you spied the orange toy. You put it away. Thank you! You know your colors!"

- Play Freeze Cleanup. Play music while children work with the goal of the game to finish cleaning up by the time the music stops. To increase interest, stop and start the music periodically. Children freeze when the music stops. (Note: The faster the music, the more quickly children will move. However, if putting things in their proper places neatly is your goal, play music that is bright and energetic but not too fast. Vivaldi's *Four Seasons* might be a good choice.)

• Challenge children to move in a different way as they clean up. "Let's all walk on tip-toe (or stomp or slide or march) today while we clean up!" "Clap your hands every time you put a toy away!"

• Challenge children to find and count five things that need to be put away. For older children, repeat the challenge increasing the number by one or two each time.

Songs

Singing a simple song effectively signals cleanup time and acknowledges children as they work.

• Sing these words to the tune of "The Farmer in the Dell": "It's time to clean our room, it's time to clean our room. Hi-ho, the derry-oh, it's time to clean our room." Then as you see children work, sing: "Dayna's picking up, Dayna's picking up. She's picking up the blocks and cars; Dayna's picking up." Or sing: "I see Eli work, I see Eli work. He's cleaning up our living room; I see Eli work." A song that includes a child's name and how he or she is helping works wonders!

• Sing these words to the tune of "Mary Had a Little Lamb": "Now we're going to clean our room, clean our room, clean our room. Now we're going to clean our room and then it's time for (snack, naps, lunch, the yard, etc.)!" Acknowledge a child's actions by singing "Shelby's helping clean our room, clean our room, clean our room. Shelby's helping clean our room and then she'll have a snack!" This tells children what comes next and helps them see cleaning up as part of getting ready for the next activity.

• Sing the same song as a cleanup signal every time. This auditory cue helps children transition. When adequate time is scheduled, children need not hurry, running madly to throw things into boxes. Rather, they can move slowly enough to stop and appreciate the neat results of what they are doing!

Cleaning Up Needs Storage

When a room has low shelves for storage of toys, games, puzzles and blocks, children's eyes are drawn to the shapes and colors of equipment. Choosing a shape of block or finding a particular toy is less frustrating.

• Use bins only for small toys. Have a separate bin for each kind of small toy, so children can sort toys as they put them into the bins. Mark the side of the bin with a picture of what belongs inside to help children sort items. (Cut pictures from the boxes the items came in!)

• When children remove blocks from block shelves, it's best to keep free floor space, so others have access to blocks. Lay a masking-tape line about three feet from the block shelves. Instruct children to build only on the side away from the shelves.

• Puzzle racks are available at most school supply stores. Encourage any child who uses a puzzle to put all the pieces back in place and set the puzzle back on the rack. (Mark the back of each puzzle piece with the same number or symbol or draw outlines of puzzle pieces on the puzzle boards, so you can quickly put puzzle pieces together if needed.)

Cleaning up is worth the time, worth the effort of making it fun and worth having appropriate places in which to store items. This makes cleaning up an enjoyable part of the routine, instead of a reason to whine. (This does not guarantee a neat bedroom when a child grows into a teenager, however!)

Disabilities: Caring for Special Needs Children in the Classroom

Our primary role as teachers is to build relationships with the young children we teach. Although content is important, relationship is what *connects* a child to the content of biblical truth! The love and nurturing any child receives sends a strong message about God's love and about your relationship with God.

Building relationships with children whose abilities are not like those of their classmates requires extra work. It requires extra planning and thoughtfulness, driven by extra compassion. Consistently making every child feel fully accepted is truly showing the kind of love Jesus showed. No matter how much care may be required of us, Jesus stands ready to give us creative solutions to problems and make us able to love and accept each child He brings to us. We need only to ask!

Attitudes

Adult Attitudes

Is a child with a special need a problem to be solved—or a person to be enjoyed? When you meet a child with a disability, focus on getting to know and enjoy him or her, rather than on managing possible problems. It will make a tremendous difference in your attitude!

If you find it difficult to be completely gracious and loving to a child with a disability, admit your need. Ask God to give you His love. Find a helper who is comfortable with the child. Invite the parents to observe during a class session with you to give you feedback as to how you can best help their child.

Children's Attitudes

Children readily absorb adult attitudes. And children best remember the attitudes we show in our unguarded moments! When we live out patience and unconditional acceptance, calmness and a nonjudgmental attitude, children will follow suit.

If another child seems afraid of a child with a disability or refuses to play with him or her, pair the disabled child with someone who is comfortable with him or her. Quietly take the first child aside to gently find out what his or her fear or worry is. Deal with the child's concerns. When the child understands the situation, he or she is likely to become one of the disabled child's staunch allies. Your job is not to force acceptance but to model it!

Children with disabilities will likely be unable to participate in some class activities. It may also require extra help to keep them involved. Specifically assign a helper to only one or two disabled children to provide the extra attention they need. Practical suggestions for helping children with specific disabilities follow.

Types of Disabilities
Communication

Especially at younger ages, many children cannot make a full range of speech sounds. This is quite common and it is usually not difficult to understand a child's meaning. But when a child has difficulty producing many sounds, people feel uncomfortable about asking the child to repeat something he or she said. Don't pretend to understand. It frustrates the child to ask a specific question and get a vague answer! The best policy is to ask the child to repeat his or her words. If the next attempt is still not clear, ask the child to act out the sentence or point at the object he or she needs. The goal is to be honest with the child, respect him or her and show that even if you don't understand the words, he or she is important and someone you want to understand. Talk with the parents to get tips on how to best communicate with their child.

Describing a child's actions in words helps language learning take place. "Lia, you are building a tower. I see a red block on top, a blue block in the middle and a green one on the bottom."

(Tip: If you cannot understand a child's words, ask the other children to listen and tell you what was said. Children often understand other children better than an adult does!)

Hearing

Children who are hard of hearing are as diverse as children who hear normally. A hearing deficit does not have any relation to intellectual ability! There are a variety of ways that deaf children communicate: reading lips, using sign language, acting out ideas or enhancing hearing with hearing aids can all be part of a child's total communication.

If a child's main means of communication is signing, have the parents teach you some basic signs for keywords you'll use during class ("hello," "Jesus," "God," "love," "please," "thank you," etc.). You'll quickly see that the other children in class will enjoy learning the signs as well! This includes everyone in understanding the deaf child. Books and websites offering sign language information abound. Take the opportunity to add this new dimension to your class!

Hearing aids can be both a help and hindrance. (They can be turned off!) Ask the parents to show you how the child's hearing aid works. Because hearing aids amplify *all* sounds, remember that a hearing-impaired child will probably not seem to understand a person talking at the front of a noisy room. Speaking naturally and not too quickly will help a child read lips. Be sure the child is looking at you before you begin to speak.

If other children are interested in the child's hearing aid, explain that hearing aids help people hear like glasses help people see.

(Tip: Rephrasing and restating information is especially helpful for the child who needs further clarification.)

Visual

Visual difficulties are more rare among young children, so they are sometimes met with greater curiosity. When other children ask questions, invite the child to answer questions if he or she would like to. Explain, "Ryan is wearing a patch over one eye for a while so that his eyes will learn to see better." When you are accepting and matter-of-fact, children are likely to follow your example.

Treat a visually impaired child as you would any child. Apply the same rules and encourage the child to do as much as he or she can. Depending on the degree of vision, most children can participate fully in class. When it is necessary to see posters or other visual aids, let the child sit close to you or bring the item close to the child's face. Invite other children to take turns walking with the child around the room. Encourage both children to touch various items and describe what they touch. This will help sighted children understand what it is like to have partial or no vision.

Visually impaired children also will benefit from your verbal descriptions. "I see you are playing blocks with Ashley. That tower is tall!" To include the visually impaired child and to model ways for other children to connect with the child, describe pictures, actions you see around the room and what you see out the window.

(Tip: Remember that visually impaired children need gentle touches from you if they are not able to see the visual cues you might give [smiles, pointing, etc.]. Touch them as often as you would smile at them!)

Physical

Whatever a child's physical disability, talk to parents when the child first joins your class. Find out how parents prefer you explain their child's disability. Describe the activities of a normal class session and ask parents to give you feedback on ways their child can participate. Invite the parents to observe or help with a class session, so they can share ways to best help the child participate. Your goal is to focus on the child's abilities, not disabilities, as you gather this information.

If a child has a severe physical disability, recruit a regular volunteer as that child's helper. Quite often people who are overwhelmed being with a group of children are happy to minister to the needs of one child.

Because building relationships and sharing God's love are the most important parts of your teaching, be alert to ways to adapt an activity to best include the disabled child. That child's presence and participation will broaden the experience of the whole class. As the child senses your love and acceptance, he or she will learn what God's love is like!

Mental and Developmental

Mental or developmental disabilities (Down's Syndrome, cerebral palsy, autism, etc.) have many different causes, degrees and layers of complexity. Remember that no matter the disability, each child is unique. Some children may be extremely affectionate. Others may not want to interact. Accepting each child and his or her unique behaviors will make a positive difference both for the child and for his or her entire family.

Children with Down's Syndrome or other developmental disabilities often have characteristics of children younger than their chronological age. They have much shorter attention spans than others of their age and often are not able to pick up on the social cues that help them relate to other children. Encourage these children with what they can do. Give hugs, touches and verbal praise to communicate your loving acceptance.

Greet a mentally disabled child and the child's parent warmly. Communicate clearly to the parents that you are delighted that their child comes to your class. Parents of children with developmental disabilities are often shunned. They rarely hear comments other parents may hear often, such as "What a beautiful child!" Talk positively about the child to the parents. Yours may be the only positive feedback the parents receive.

Take time to talk with the parents about the child's strengths and any concerns the parents have. Then encourage the child to use his or her strengths in your class. If needed, recruit an additional helper to spend time with the child. During class, that helper can watch for signs of frustration or restlessness and be prepared to help the child or begin another activity with the child.

If other children ask what is wrong with the child, answer simply and honestly. (Check with the child's parents to be sure you have correct information and terminology about the disability.) Most preschoolers are not interested in lengthy explanations. "Dana's feet don't work like your feet do. But she can do lots of other things. Would you and Dana like to help me with this puzzle?" Focus on the child's abilities, instead of the disabilities. Describe ways children can help the disabled child and each other.

(Tip: Remember that a mentally disabled child's family is probably under some stress! Parents may be blaming the disability on themselves or each other. A parent's dreams for this child may have been shattered. Knowing the child may never be able to live independently can be overwhelming. Brothers and sisters of disabled children may be under unusual stress to be good or help out. Your gentle, positive approach and genuine acceptance help all family members feel loved and supported.)

ADD and ADHD

Attention Deficit Disorder (ADD) and Attention Deficit Hyperactivity Disorder (ADHD) are an increasingly common part of dealing with school-aged children. Because most of the behaviors found in ADD and ADHD are a normal part of preschool behavior, it is not usually seen as a problem for young children. However, medicating younger children is becoming more

common. Whatever your feelings about the issue, give each child as much of a matter-of-fact, accepting attitude as you do with any other special need. Always focus on what the child *can* do and how to best adapt to and include him or her.

During circle times, seat these children near you. Incorporate a variety of activities (especially hands-on activities) and expect them to participate as fully as they can. Don't be afraid to set and enforce a few behavior expectations. "Keep hands and feet to yourself. Listen when others talk." Your loving acceptance will send the message that each child is important, loved and accepted *as is*, not as the child might be. As one wise teacher said, "God put the wiggles in children. It's not up to us to take them out!"

(Tip: Plan learning activities that the child enjoys and that allow for lots of interaction with others. Have on hand a variety of sensory items [soft stuffed animal, smooth stone, etc.] for a child to hold during large-group times.)

Final Focus

Take stock. Acknowledge your own level of discomfort in dealing with a child who is disabled and his or her family. Then consider the ways in which Jesus responded to disabled people!

Parents and families of disabled children often feel isolated and desperately need friends who will love and accept them *and* their children. They need people who will welcome them into their homes and who will go places with them. They need people who will listen and pray while they rage against what seems to be God's great unfairness. Accepting a child with a disability into your class can be the beginning of healing a whole family. God promises to give wisdom as you ask in faith. He will supply patience as you pray. He wants to help you pass on His healing love!

Discipline: Goals and Methods for Guiding Young Children

Definition and Goal

It's common to hear an adult say in exasperation, "What that child needs is some discipline!" It's true that a young child's behavior might frustrate us. It's also true that every adult, parent and teacher has expectations of how a child should act. But it is very important that we understand first what discipline is.

One meaning of "discipline" is "training that corrects, molds and makes complete or perfect." Let's look to Jesus for a definition of "discipline." What did Jesus do to correct and mold adults (who often did not live up to His expectations) and bring them to a place of maturity? Jesus chose *disciples* who would be *disciplined,* or trained, by Him. His goal for their training was for them to become mature in Him, ready to take His Word all over the world. How did He train them? By giving out punishment? By making rules? No. He did it by living with them! Jesus gave them a walking, talking, breathing, listening example of what He wanted them to become. He taught more often by action and attitude than even by word. Most of the disciples' time with Jesus was spent observing and then doing.

What is our goal, then, for the discipline of our children? Good discipline is not what we do to a child but what we do with and for him or her. We guide a child to help him or her grow toward self-control in knowing and doing what is good. We give loving guidance to establish a positive atmosphere for learning!

Methods

"Love me and accept me as I am." Such love gives a child what he or she needs to grow and develop. Children long to feel that someone cares about them and that they are people of worth and value. When a child enters the room, put yourself at his or her eye level. Listen attentively to what a child has to tell. When a child's behavior is out of bounds, kindly redirect the child. Phrase your directions positively: tell the child what he or she *may* do, instead of what he or she may *not* do. Rather than scold or shame a child, focus on the child's behavior. "Chris, we keep the dough on the table. You may pick up what is on the floor. Then you may choose what kind of animal you'd like to make. I see Kelly is making a snake."

Telling Chris he is a bad boy or giving him a list of reasons why we don't throw dough will not help him refocus and choose ways to change. Kindness, clear directions and choices within limits will help any child learn good discipline!

"If you do it, I will do it, too." Children watch constantly. If they hear you talk about how important it is to pick up trash but see you drop paper on the ground, expect that they will drop paper, too. The actions you do, teach far more than the words you say.

"Let me know what is coming next." Young children thrive on the security that comes from knowing the routine. "After we clean up the blocks, we will have our story." Keeping the same order during every class session helps make young children feel calm and secure. Variety is the spice of life, but it is best used sparingly with young children. One surprise a day is plenty!

"Give me choices to make." Provide a

variety of interesting things for children to do. When children have a choice of activities, they are much more likely to be interested in the activity and are far less likely to create discipline problems; too many choices can have the same detrimental effect. "Tawny, you may make a picture, build with blocks or dress up in the drama corner."

"Give me a place to work." If you expect children to work and move without bumping into each other, be sure your room provides enough space to work. Can the room be rearranged so that children can move more easily? What can be cleaned up or discarded so that the room has adequate space for each child?

Responses to Unacceptable Behaviors

With all of our best work and most loving intentions, there will still be those moments when a child misbehaves in a way that requires immediate verbal intervention. For young children, we have only about 10 seconds to correct the behavior in any way that will have meaning for them.

Hitting or Kicking: "Rina, kicking hurts. I cannot let you hurt Dylan. Use words to tell Dylan what you want." Separate the children. Comfort Dylan briefly, and then help Rina move to another activity if need be. Stay with her until she is involved.

Biting: Biting may be motivated by curiosity with very young preschoolers or by frustration and anger as children get older. (Most children know biting is not OK by the time they are around three.) "Biting hurts. We don't hurt other people. We use our teeth for chewing food." Comfort the one bitten and let an adult helper clean the wound and fill out a report. Separate the children. NEVER encourage the one bitten to bite back. It won't help the biter and will create many more problems!

Using Offensive Words: "In our class, we use kind words. That is not a kind word.

Alex is building a good tower. You're building a good tower, too." When you say kind words to the verbal offender, you let that child know that you care about him or her regardless of the behavior. That teaches kindness very effectively!

Having a Tantrum: If there is no response to words, hold the child firmly but gently until he or she calms down. Holding the child offers protection as well as control. If other children are frightened by the tantrum, let an adult helper gently take the tantrum-thrower to another room while you briefly explain what is happening. "Kerry is having a hard time. She will be OK soon."

Distracting Others: We all like attention. Most of what human beings do is designed to get attention from another person! When a child is distracting others who are trying to listen, ask a helper to sit beside the child. Sometimes just a touch or an arm around the shoulders will refocus the child. Always make behavior the child's choice. "Tim, if you want to stay in the circle by Jon, you will need to stop kicking your feet. You can sit pretzel style or sit with your legs in front of you." Now there is a choice to be made. The decision is up to Tim. Give a child time to adjust. If Tim continues to kick, say, "Tim, I see you are still kicking. You need to move away from Jon now. You need to sit by Miss Emily." Signal your helper to move the child next to her. When you have simply and positively stated what needs to happen, follow through with the consequences you stated if the child doesn't change behavior.

If more than one child is showing signs of restlessness, recognize that it is time for a change of pace! Stand up, stretch, do a quick finger fun activity or sing a song. Young children's muscles quickly grow tired in one position. Everyone will be better able to sit still if sitting times are not too long!

When we remember the goals of discipline, the methods of discipline and the power of our own example, discipline becomes the positive tool it is designed to be.

Dramatic Play Center: Acting Out Everyday Life

The dramatic play area provides a place where young children can pretend to be anyone they want to be! Children can go from simply experimenting with costumes and props to fully re-creating their world in any way they can imagine it! It enables children to practice the social roles and activities they see around them.

Characteristics of Play

Social Interaction: Two or more children within the group talk about what they will play. They take on roles and then interact in that context. They may often transform an object into another use (a spatula becomes a microphone) or do an imaginary action (moving hands in ways to symbolize eating).

Verbal Communication: Children talk naturally as part of the pretending. The teacher stays alert nearby, watching for times when he or she can make a comment that helps to extend thinking, make predictions, try new ideas or relate children's actions to the Bible words or focus of the day's lesson.

Levels of Play

A child's interest and activity in dramatic play reflect his or her level of development. Most children under three are likely to simply rock a baby, pretend to *be* the baby or play alongside other children, rarely involving anyone else in their activities. Since their ability to use words is limited, they often use play as a way to express ideas. As children grow through their third, fourth and fifth years, imaginative play becomes more and more complex. As children mature, they learn to interact with other children and often adopt the roles of family members. They spend longer periods of time in imaginative play and enjoy using costumes and props such as household items, adult clothing and accessories. They also enjoy playing out the roles of community helpers: mail carriers, firefighters, doctors, etc.

Teachable Moments

When children are playing out everyday situations, there are many opportunities to act out kindness, forgiveness and patience. Don't assume you are not needed in this setting. Your role is vitally important. And it's simple! Get to know each child. Ask open-ended questions ("What do you think will happen if . . .?" "How do you think we can solve . . .?") as children play. Your simple suggestions can help them see solutions to problems, help them understand ways to be kind or share and can help them see how the day's Bible verse applies to real life. If children's play seems to stall, ask a question or two to help give them new ideas.

Always be alert for those moments when you can make a brief comment on how a child's action reflects the day's lesson focus or Bible verse. Acknowledge and encourage positive actions you see as children play! "Stephanie, I see you are sharing the cooking pots with Mara. That's a way to share and be kind, like our Bible tells us to do! Thank you!"

Acting out Bible story events (even before the story is formally told) is an ideal way for young children to learn Bible truths! It involves children's bodies as well as minds. Stories told informally this way have great impact. And since young children love repetition, hearing and acting out the Bible story more than once delights them as it reinforces Bible truth.

Basic Materials

The basic supplies needed for dramatic play activity are fairly simple: toy dishes (plates, bowls, cups and utensils), tablecloth, several washable dolls, easy-to-manage doll clothes and dress-up clothes (women's and men's). For classes of mostly young children, do not provide utensils or toy baby bottles as they will likely try to put them in their mouths. Other items to add might be toy food, doll bed, telephone, plastic jewelry, wallets, discarded camera, lunch box, briefcase, ties and scarves.

Costume and Prop Boxes

Children may not especially enjoy it when adults dress them up, but they do love to dress up when they are provided with a variety of interesting clothing items and props! While basic dress-up items and props should be available in the dramatic play area all the time, rotate other items to keep dramatic play interesting.

To effectively rotate extra props and clothing, organize them by themes such as Bible times, grocery store, mail carrier, gardening, mechanic, restaurant, baby care, etc. Gather costumes and props for each theme into clear plastic boxes or large boxes with lids (office paper boxes work well). Label boxes. Regularly launder and clean all props and clothing.

Easter: Making Easter Joyful

Children learn about Easter in some interesting ways! They are exposed to videos (both religious and secular), photo opportunities with the Easter Bunny in the mall, traditional family gatherings, community egg hunts and ads for Easter clothing, Easter baskets and candy. This celebratory mixture is bound to confuse children! Even for adults, it's sometimes hard to separate the traditions from the truths. Jesus' death and resurrection is the single most powerful and important chain of events in human history. But it is easy to focus on the fun and yet miss the joy. Easter is far more than the trappings that surround the holiday!

Keep It Simple

Long after Easter day is passed, it's important that children understand and remember that Jesus is alive! As adults, we need to keep in mind that words and phrases that are quite clear to us often have little meaning for young children. Young children have very vague and uneasy notions about death. While this truth is vitally important to our faith, "Jesus died and rose again" is not likely to be clear or seem like a reason to be excited and happy! (*What does dying have to do with a flower? Why are you glad that Jesus died? I was sad when my Grandma died.*)

Instead of dwelling on the details of Christ's death, help children grasp the great truth of the Easter story—that Jesus took the punishment for our sin and that He did not stay dead. He is alive now! Help them understand how Jesus' friends felt: "Jesus' friends were very sad when Jesus died. They were sad because they thought they would never see Jesus again. When they found out that Jesus did not stay dead, they must have laughed and hugged each other! They told everyone they knew, 'Jesus is alive again! Jesus is living! We saw Him!'"

As you talk, show pictures (from a Bible storybook, for example) that are clear and help children understand what you are telling. Ask them open-ended questions, so you can find out what they know. This is your opportunity to clear up any misinformation children have picked up and build happy feelings about the Easter story. Reinforce true details about the story, rather than misconceptions children may have.

Keep It Focused

When a child talks about the Easter bunny, traditional activities or candy, simply smile and comment, "Those things are fun. But the biggest reason we are glad at Easter is because we know Jesus is alive!" In order to keep children's attention focused on the Easter story, avoid use of decorations that picture the Easter bunny. However, don't expect that children will be as excited about spiritual matters as they are about tangible things such as candy! Your excitement, enthusiasm and example in talking about Jesus' resurrection and love for us provide more understanding for young children than any extensive verbal explanation could!

Answers to Questions

As a child's ability to understand grows greater, he or she will ask more questions. Keep your answers clear and biblical.

Why did people kill Jesus?

Jesus was hurt and killed by angry people who did not like Him. They did not know that God sent Jesus to love and help everyone. Jesus let these angry people kill Him. He knew it was part of God's very good plan. Jesus knew He was going to die to take the punishment for our sin. He loves us so much that He was willing to do that. And Jesus knew He was going to be alive again!

Avoid graphic details of Jesus' death: these are better left until a child is older. If a child becomes frightened by talk of Jesus' death, he or she can be gently reminded, "It's OK. Jesus knew this was going to happen. He did not stay dead. It was part of God's good plan to make a very SAD thing into a very GLAD thing!"

Where is Jesus now?

Jesus lives in heaven now with God, His Father. Heaven is a very beautiful place. Everyone is very happy there. No one is sick or hurt there. No one cries or is sad.

What is Jesus doing in heaven?

Jesus is making a wonderful home in heaven for every person who is part of God's family. Every member of God's family will be with Him in heaven someday. Even though we can't see Him now, we know that Jesus has promised to be with us and care for us.

Families: Connecting with Families in the Twenty-First Century

"Family" means something different in every household! One family might eat home-cooked meals together daily, play games and read books together, seldom watching television. However, another family might eat together only at restaurants, rarely play games or read at all, regularly watching selections from their vast video library! The values expressed by each of these styles may be quite different, but the fact is, each family's values and style are unique. While we each hold our own set of unspoken expectations about how families should be, what are practical ways we can best connect with and support the diverse kinds of families our children represent?

grandparents and a grandchild, or two parents and one child. Family configurations have changed. However, the changes and challenges faced by families also create great opportunities! As we pray for each child, we can ask God to make us aware of the best ways to connect with that family and become agents of His grace to them. (The goal is not to interfere but to become a loving and supportive friend to every child and family, whatever the situation.)

Empathy

Where divorce or separation is part of the family situation, children are often under stresses that they themselves don't recognize. Always remember that the child had no choice in the situation. Your extra patience, nonjudgmental words and kindness are crucial! Build a bond of understanding with the child. "I hope you have fun with your mom next weekend, Rita. We'll miss you! But we'll see you on the next weekend." Your words help the child know you are on his or her side.

Awareness

Once, the family unit likely to be walking into a local church was two parents and two children. Today, the likely family unit may be one parent and three children, two

These children are also likely to be shuttled between parents, resulting in irregular attendance. If it's possible, record both parents' names, addresses and phone numbers (even if only one parent brings the child to class). When information needs to go home, be sure a copy is mailed to each parent. When a child misses the class, mail copies of his or her activity pages and take-home papers to the proper address. This will help the child feel connected with the class and will keep information flowing to both parents.

Sensitivity

As you talk about families, avoid assumptions about family life. Include references—without sounding negative—to children whose families are composed of other than traditional members. Be sensitive to children who live in a blended family or in shared custody situations. Help each child feel valued and loved. "Noah and his mom are a family. Amy and her brothers and her mom and dad are a family. Justin and his grandma and grandpa are a family. Sheena has two families. She lives with her dad and brother sometimes and lives with her sister and mom sometimes." As you explain and show acceptance, children will feel more positive and comfortable about their own families.

You may see a child's parents only when they drop off or pick up their child. It's important that you let them know you support their efforts to parent their children and teach them about God. Assign one friendly welcoming teacher or helper to the important task of greeting parents and briefly showing their child's work. For some parents, this contact may be the only conversation they have while they are at church! As you see parents' interest rise, invite them to observe the class (without pressuring them to volunteer as helpers!).

Support

Teaching young children need not end when they run out the door. No matter how busy we are, teachers of young children have unique opportunities to help young families. Our support can be something as simple as a conversation at the door that sparks an interest in an article on parenting in a take-home paper, or it can be something as involved as planning a play date event for children and parents. Young parents may be more eager to connect with each other than you expect! Mutual support and fellowship is something they need and sometimes don't have time or money to do on their own. Creating a safe place for grown-ups as well as their children is one more way you can support and love young children and their parents.

Finger Plays: Words and Actions That Teach

The joy of repetition, the fun of pretending, the bounce of following an easy rhythm with the whole body—these are all natural expressions for young children. That's the reason finger play activities (simple poems and songs with motions) are an integral part of early childhood learning! Children enjoy imagining and imitating actions. They need frequent physical breaks. Finger play offers an imaginative change of pace that gives children's large and small muscles a chance to move.

God gave young children bodies that need to wiggle and minds that have short attention spans. When young children become bored, restless or inattentive, teachers who introduce a finger play activity usually are heading off a multitude of problems! Using their bodies and minds in constructive and creative ways will help focus children's attention and help maintain a peaceful, positive atmosphere for learning.

Finger Plays to Teach Bible Truth

If children are to truly learn, they must hear the same message over and over again. With hit-or-miss attendance and ever-shortening class times, it is important that the entire Sunday School session be planned to accomplish a single set of learning goals. Each lesson is designed to weave activities together to reinforce a single set of learning goals. Because young children learn best when all of their senses are involved and they are moving physically,

using the finger play activities provided in your curriculum gives children yet another involving way to remember the Bible verse or lesson focus.

Finger Plays for Transition Times

As young children move from one part of the session to the next, finger play activities can help them make those transitions smoothly. When an alert teacher is prepared with an activity, order and calm can prevail over chaos! Finger play can draw the group together, help them focus on what is coming next, and give them the physical and mental break they need. Consider repeating the same finger play activity each session to signal a transition (such as the beginning of circle time). Children love to know what is coming next, and they enjoy knowing a finger play activity well enough to repeat it easily.

Tips for Leading Finger Plays

Practice until the activity feels natural. If the finger play is difficult for you to remember, photocopy it and post it where you can see it when facing the group of children. This way you can maintain eye contact with children even while you review the words!

Emphasize your words and speak slowly enough that children have time to respond with the actions.

Be expressive with your face and voice. This is easier to do if you have the finger play memorized.

Be realistic about participation. At first, a child may only watch. As the child becomes familiar with the finger play, encourage but never insist that he or she join in with actions and ultimately with words.

Repeat the same finger plays frequently. You may become weary of the repetition, but young children love and need the repetition.

Add interest to a familiar finger play by repeating it in a variety of ways: in a whisper, loudly, mouthing the words, etc. Invite children to make up new motions to a familiar finger play.

One, Two, Three

Stand up and turn around.
One, two, three!

Now bend and touch your toes.
One, two, three!

Reach very, very high.
One, two, three!

Now flap your wings and fly!
One, two, three!

Now sit down quietly.
One, two, three!

(Now it's time hear a story.)
One, two, three!

(Note: Substitute the task at hand for the words in parentheses.)

First Day: Welcome Each Child!

Can you remember how it felt the last time you met a roomful of people for the first time? Recalling those feelings will help you know how stressful the first day of class can be for a young child. There are, however, some ways to help a child feel welcomed and know "This is a good place to be!"

A Welcoming Environment

Your classroom is a silent partner in any child's learning experience. It can help or hinder, delight or depress! Take time to walk through your room. View it through a child's eyes. (Get down on your knees to get a child's perspective!)

Are the tables and chairs a comfortable size? Is the room light and bright? What do you notice first? Are visual aids at eye level for children? Is there a clean, comfortable place to play on the floor? Space to move freely? Does anything in the room encourage you to explore? List ways to improve the space, if needed.

Get-Acquainted Activities

Create a welcome display by printing each child's name on a sheet of construction paper. (Keep blank papers handy for guests.) Attach the papers to a bulletin board or large sheet of paper mounted on the wall. Provide a variety of fun stickers for children to put on their name papers. You may also cut pictures from catalogs or magazines that illustrate activities children will be doing (block play, dramatic play, art activities, etc.). Add these pictures to the welcome bulletin board. Talk about the pictured activities so that children know what to expect in the classroom.

As children enjoy activities on the first day, move around the room with an instant camera. Take a photo of each child, as well as photos of children playing together in small groups. Attach photos to a bulletin board or use them to mark cubby or shelf space for each child. Display group photos at eye level for children to enjoy. This creates a sense of being included!

Invite older children to bring an item from home to share on the first day. This provides a comforting object to hold as well as something for each child to talk about and help children get to know each other.

First Day Reactions

Sometimes children are overexcited on the first day. This can result in needing to use the bathroom more often, wetting or vomiting. While these small emergencies may be a trial to you, it's important that you respond calmly, kindly and with understanding. A child needs to know he or she is accepted, no matter what!

Keep a small stock of both boys' and girls' clothing in several sizes in case a child needs clean clothing.

Always show children where the bathroom is for the first few sessions. If a child wets, respond positively. "It's OK. We'll clean you up now. Remember, you can tell me any time you need to go to the bathroom. I'll be happy to take you right away."

Game Center: It's Fun to Play and Learn

Games for young children are not the same kinds of games that older children or adults play. For young children, games are more like organized guided play. They may involve exploring, combining and manipulating materials. Other games may involve movement, simple responses or recalling information while enjoying activity and feeling included.

For young children, games need to be involving (that means very little time spent waiting for a turn!). Games need to be easygoing and noncompetitive. They should not involve a long list of rules. A young child may follow rules for a while, but as excitement builds, the rules often slip away! The focus of a game for young children is on the fun of doing, not on winning. Such games need no winners or losers, for the excitement of meeting the challenge in the game is enough.

Age-Level Characteristics

Two- and three-year-olds enjoy the challenge of matching colors, shapes or sizes of items and pictures. Movement games for younger ones include rolling a ball, dropping clothespins into a container, tossing a

beanbag into a bucket, playing Follow the Leader or Simon Says (without anyone ever being out). Such games are easily adapted to the children's developmental level. Playing the game in more than one way helps develop thinking skills and heightens interest.

Four- and five-year-olds are able to play simple board games and concentration games with a limited number of game pieces. Increase the challenge in skill games such as tossing a beanbag by moving the target or inviting children to toss the beanbag in a different way (with both hands, under a leg, etc.). Use lightweight balls to play simple toss-and-catch games. Bowl to knock over plastic two-liter bottles. Push lightweight balls along the floor with plastic baseball bats or brooms.

With young children, expect to play a game over and over again. Young children love repetition because repeating an activity helps them gain experience and skill. Feeling successful and competent should be one goal of any game!

The Playing Area

Plan what you will need to do to create a playing area within your classroom. You may need to move unneeded furniture or rearrange chairs or tables. If necessary for certain games, mark boundaries with yarn, masking tape or painter's tape. (Be sure to remove masking tape from floor after each session.) If you have little space in your classroom in which to play games, consider alternatives: outdoor areas, a hallway or a gymnasium.

Basic Materials

Some games require no materials at all. Other games require items that can be found in most classrooms or homes. The following supplies can be used in many games: beanbags, several soft balls in various sizes, butcher paper, markers, masking tape (or painter's tape) and yarn, colored construction paper and scissors.

Guided Conversation

Using guided conversation turns a game activity into discovery learning! Make use of the conversation suggestions provided in your curriculum. These conversation starters will help you relate the child's activity to the lesson. Keep in mind the lesson focus and Bible verse for each lesson. Then your natural conversation can tie children's activities to the lesson's Bible truths. Some games may connect directly to Bible story action. Briefly telling parts of the Bible story can help make the connection.

Get Acquainted: Know the Children You Teach

Early Childhood Questionnaire

Child's Name

Birth Date

Address

Phone

Father's Name

Mother's Name

Siblings and Ages

Ask children the following questions to familiarize yourself with their interests and to help you plan effective learning activities:

1. What's your favorite toy or game at your house?

2. What is your favorite animal?

3. What do you like to play outside?

4. Who do you like to play with?

5. What do you like to do with your family? With your friends?

6. Where do you like to go?

7. What do you like to do at Sunday School?

Giving Directions: Quick Ideas for Getting Children's Attention

When it's time to give directions or get children's attention, children may be told "Sit still until everyone is here" or "Wait in line until we are ready." Such methods of gaining attention and control are self-defeating if we are trying to teach kindness and respect through our own behavior. They also create negative feelings and waste valuable teaching time. There are better ways!

When You Want to Start

It's easy to establish a simple attention-getting signal for the children in your class. Choose a signal to use and introduce the signal with spoken directions. It's a good idea to practice using the signal until the children are familiar with it. Once children know the routine, simply give the signal and allow children time to respond. Always acknowledge and thank children by name who respond quickly to the signal. Here are a few signal ideas:

• Flick lights on and off two or three times.

• Slowly count aloud to five to see if everyone can be quietly looking at you before you say "five."

• Hold up two fingers (or hold up a different number of fingers each time) and invite children whose attention you've gained to tell how many fingers you are holding up.

• Sing the same song or play the same music before the same activity at each session. "By the time the song is finished, you should all be sitting on the floor."

• Ring a bell. (Collect several different bells. Make a game of identifying which bell you rang.)

• Clap hands in a pattern. Children imitate pattern as you gain their attention.

• Say "One, two, three—all eyes on me." (Follow this with a question: "What color is my sweater?" or "What animal do you think is on the back of my shirt?")

• Use a finger play poem or other chant for children to imitate. (Change finger plays to keep interest high, but do the same one consistently for a while, so children know that finger play is a signal.)

• As children gather, sing a song that includes each of their names. Others will hurry to join you to hear their names sung!

While Children Listen

There are times during a circle time or story time when some children lose interest. Plan ahead for these times! When restlessness runs high, try these ideas:

• Ask a question, using a child's name.

• Whisper your words, which often generates renewed interest from children.

• Change the pace by leading children in a finger play, an action song or a simple imitation game to recall attention.

• If you are using a visual aid or a book, invite children to put hands on their heads when they see an item in the picture. Then return to the story without further comment.

Always phrase directions to even the most wiggly child in terms of what he or she can do, instead of what not to do. "Ryan, you need to sit on the floor. I'm looking to see if you can put your hands on your knees like mine. Thank you!"

How to Get Your Message Across

Here are some tips for effective communication with young children:

• Get the child's attention before speaking. Adults waste lots of breath saying things when no one is listening. For example, shouting across a room to a child results in confusion, rather than communication. Go to the child. Bend down so that your face is at his or her eye level. Speak the child's name. "Seth, it's time for you to put the markers in the can."

• Say the most important words first. After you've spoken the child's name, briefly state what you want the child to do. Then you may add a reason. "Karla, put your paper by the door. It's almost time for your dad to come."

• Use simple words and a natural tone of voice. Speak slowly and distinctly in a soft, yet audible, tone. Let your voice express your enthusiasm and interest. Add a smile to your words. Avoid baby talk or gushing.

• Use specific words. General terms leave a child confused, not knowing exactly what you mean. Rather than "Put the toys away," say, "Alex, your red truck needs to go here on this shelf."

Guided Conversation: Making the Connection Between the Bible and Life

Why do we need to guide conversation with young children? Don't we simply talk to them? Certainly there are many times when simple conversation is spontaneous. However, guided conversation helps children remember and recognize ways to apply the Bible truth that is the foundation for the day's activities.

What is guided conversation? Does it mean the teacher spends every minute spouting Bible verses or repeating the day's lesson focus? Talking only when a problem arises? No! Guided conversation is simply informal but planned conversation in which the teacher looks for opportunities to connect what children are doing to the Bible learning content of the session. Relating the child's activities to Bible truths helps the child understand the relationship between what he or she is doing and what the Bible says.

 **Step One: Know the session's lesson focus and Bible verse.** This prepares you to share these ideas whenever natural opportunities and teachable moments occur.

 **Step Two: Listen.** The biggest part of being a skilled teacher is being a good listener. When children are absorbed in an activity or are playing together, don't take a break or leave the area. Place yourself at the children's eye level, available to hear. Listening and observing provides you with helpful insight into each child's thoughts and feelings. Watch and listen for clues to their interests, how they see themselves and what things might bother them. Resist the temptation to tune a child out or race ahead mentally.

 **Step Three: Ask questions.** Invite children into conversation that involves more than answering yes or no. Ask open-ended questions that invite the child to describe and discuss! For instance, when you see a child stacking blocks, you could say, "What do you think will happen if you put this big block on top? This little block?" Or you could say, "Tell me about your construction." Questions and comments that cannot be answered with a yes or no help children learn verbal skills, help them express their feelings and give you greater insight into their thoughts and feelings.

 **Step Four: Relate the child's thoughts and feelings to God's Word!** You might begin by commenting on what you see. "Sheena, you helped Jake! You are obeying our Bible verse. God tells us to help each other. Thank you!" You may also rephrase a child's words. "It sounds like you had a happy time with Delia, Mike. Our Bible tells us God gives us friends. We can thank God for Delia. Thank You, God, for Mike's friend Delia!"

When you identify acts of kindness or helpfulness, children then learn what it means to help each other, share or take turns. Relate a child's actions immediately, before children forget the circumstances. And use the child's name. Often, a child who does not hear his or her name assumes you are talking to someone else!

As you see children experience satisfaction, curiosity or even frustration, you are witnessing teachable moments. Children are especially receptive to new ideas at such times. Step in with a comment or question that will help the child resolve the problem; affirm a child's accomplishment with an "I see . . ." comment; answer a child's question and thank God for the child's curiosity on the spot!

With the session's Bible truths in mind, you are ready to listen, observe and comment in ways that will help each child understand more about how God's love and God's Word relate to his or her world.

Kindergartners: Increasing the Challenge

In any group of children entering kindergarten, developmental maturity might range from that of a three-year-old to that of a seven-year-old. This is neither good nor bad—it simply *is*. Every child develops at his or her own unique pace. Because of such differences, teachers need to be ready to either simplify or expand activities in such a way that every child gains understanding, competence and feelings of success.

At some point during the kindergarten year, many children's minds seem to suddenly kick into high gear. Fascinated with learning, they ask wonderful questions that show they are thinking deeply: "Where is heaven? Why does the water look blue? What makes your brain think?" These children are eager for greater mental challenges. Here are basic ways to expand activities and increase the challenge, keeping every child excited and involved!

Thinking Skills

Any activity, at any moment, can be given an increasing level of challenge.

• Invite children to observe and then categorize. "What is the same about these pumpkins and these watermelons? What is different?" "What other fruits are the same color as these apples?" "How many sheep do you see in the picture?" "How many horses with brown spots do you count? How many goats have black tails?"

• Invite children to find common characteristics either in something or someone observed. "Who else is wearing red?" "Where is another person in the picture who is wearing a sweater?" "What are Arcelia and I wearing that is the same?"

• Stop at various points when reading a story and invite children to predict what they think will happen next. To expand the prediction work, invite children to make up endings to the story or draw a picture of what they think could happen next, or invite children to suggest outcomes if a character did something different. "What would have been different if Jesus had told the blind man to be quiet?" "What if Samuel had not asked Eli what he wanted?"

• Begin an open-ended story. Invite each child to take a turn contributing one or two sentences. You may also show a picture and ask children to tell what they think happened before the picture or what they think might happen next. Such simple activities

challenge and sharpen thinking skills.

• Change an item of your clothing slightly and challenge children to detect what was changed.

• Play charade games of any kind. Charades help children to learn the nuances of body language and think of ways to communicate without words.

Word Skills

Take advantage of children's natural curiosity regarding words and reading in the natural situations that arise during class time.

• When children are asked to name people whom they can help, print the names on a large sheet of paper.

• As part of a prayer time, ask children to name items for which they are thankful. Print each word on a large sheet of paper. "Read" the list aloud after each child has contributed.

• If children in your class are beginning readers, print the words of a Bible verse on separate cards. As each word of the verse is said aloud, give a child the appropriate card. Then ask children to place the cards in order.

• Label classroom items, so interested children may read the names.

While it is impressive when a young child can recite a Bible passage, memorization is no guarantee of understanding. Adult approval for memorizing will likely make a child feel successful but may also send the message that Bible words are just phrases to be spoken, not God's Word that gives direction to our lives. If children are to memorize Scripture, it should be a verse whose meaning you can make clear. Help them understand what they are repeating. If you are not able to make the ideas in the passage clear to the children, perhaps that passage should be left for later!

Since a kindergarten-aged class usually contains children not yet reading, children in the process of learning to read and beginning readers, incorporate activities that include children at any skill level. Give children books to "read" to each other (whether or not the actual words are read); let them listen to recordings of a story while looking at books that contain the same words. These kinds of enrichment will help to span the gap in reading skills among children.

Number Skills

Counting anything is fun for kindergartners!

• Teach the names of the first five numbers in a foreign language.

• Measure items with a measuring tape or measuring stick.

• Use Post-it Notes to add and subtract items from a picture.

• Bring a scale and weigh a variety of items.

• Invite children to sort manipulative items (small building blocks, large beads, plastic animals, etc.) into a variety of categories, or create patterns in the way items are placed on the table or floor.

Include these challenges in such a way that children feel it is simply good fun. They are learning far more by these simple experiences than we can classify! Don't, however, test them later or expect right answers.

The heart of these expansion ideas is not so much achieving specific educational goals as much as it is stimulating children to explore and discover, keeping their involvement high. Most of all, make learning challenges fun! Don't pressure children to perform. Simply play with them, give out information and remind them of God's love for each one. Express your gratitude to God for the abilities He gave them!

Learning Styles: Understanding Each Child's Strengths

To be the most effective teachers or parents we can be, we need to be aware of a child's style of learning. God made each of us unique and loves our uniqueness. Once we understand styles of learning, we are better able to provide an environment that helps children know the reality of God's love for each of them as individuals!

Research is constantly finding new ways people learn and express their knowledge. As you read the broad descriptions of these ways given below, first recognize your own learning styles: these affect the choices for activities you plan. Then read again to pinpoint the strengths of the young learners you know. Most children will display a combination of these approaches to learning.

Visual

Visual learners learn best when there is something to look at. They enjoy creating pictures and building with blocks. They usually are eager to learn to read and write because they want to see the information. They like to imagine the scenes of the stories they hear, enjoy worksheets and prefer complete quiet to background music or sound. They are bothered by visual clutter, so they prefer an orderly environment. (It's estimated that most school teachers are mainly visual learners!)

Verbal/Auditory

Verbal learners learn best by talking and conversing. They process ideas as they talk about them; they like to listen to stories read aloud or audio versions of books. They remember things that are set to music. They like to have music or sound in the background and are not very bothered by visual clutter. They ask many questions, not because they weren't paying attention, but because they want more understanding. They may be considered too talkative or distracting, but verbal youngsters challenge us to provide those opportunities to talk and listen so that they can learn!

Physical/Tactile

Physical learners learn best when their bodies are in motion. They often have good coordination and may use their hands as they talk or may act out what they say. They process information with their whole bodies! Tactile learners learn well through touch. They like to take things apart. They fiddle with things constantly and learn far more by doing than by seeing or hearing. Physical and tactile learners respond to touches and hugs, a cozy environment and soft lighting. They need lots of hands-on activities that involve more than one sense. Large-muscle activities (such as an action to help them remember a word, etc.) help keep these children involved.

Relational/Reflective

Relational learners are keen observers, noting body language and tone of voice. They process information by realizing how people feel and they respond accordingly. They like cooperative, interactive activities; they are "people persons" who are energized by interaction.

Reflective learners don't shun group activities, but they tend to think more about who they are and where they fit; they are sometimes drained by too much group interaction and express themselves more often through one-person activities.

Logical

To some degree, every child is a problem-solver and explorer, but some take to it and enjoy it more than others. These learners see the patterns in the world and can think through problems. They are glad to have point-by-point explanations of how things work and enjoy games and puzzles that challenge them. They often count things without being asked to count. They may enjoy sorting toys into categories (things that are red, things that fly, etc.).

Musical

Most young children enjoy music, but some are more sensitive to rhythm and pitch and to the musical quality of spoken language (such as poetry). They tend to be good listeners but probably won't sit still when music is playing: they express themselves through making up songs of their own on the spot and through dance and movement whenever they hear music.

This brief overview describes some of the ways all humans process new information. When you provide activities that challenge and stimulate children in the ways they learn best, they are more focused and ready to learn. It may not be easy or interesting for you to do some activities because of your own learning styles. But as you understand the needs of each child, you'll find it worthwhile to try the activities you never thought you'd do.

Mixed Ages: Teaching a Group of Twos Through Fives

There are times when one class of preschool-aged children may range from two years to five or six years of age. It's important for a teacher of any class containing such a large developmental span to be well prepared! Such varied levels of development require that a teacher tailor some activities so that each child learns best at his or her own level of development.

To a degree, younger children will enjoy being with the "big kids" and will be attracted to the activities in which older children are involved. Generally speaking, however, the younger the child, the more easily he or she will be distracted. Therefore, the younger child needs more direct,

firsthand activity for effective learning. So that all activities need not be set at the level of the very youngest ones, divide the class into older and younger groups as time and helpers allow. If materials are used with older children that are not suitable for use by younger children, provide careful supervision at all times.

Use the activity center method. Keep at least one helper or teacher with each group to observe and talk with children. As you rotate these groups through the centers, let every child work at his or her own pace. Keep in mind that younger children have shorter attention spans and are likely to move between activities more frequently. Older children will be able to focus longer.

If some children don't stay in their age-related groups, don't panic. Such a natural adjustment is probably best! As teachers and helpers get to know each child, they can be observant as children interact. They will then be better able to adjust members, times and activities for any group as needed.

Plan to use activities that are open-ended. When children are all expected to produce the same craft item, the activity will require a great deal of adult intervention (and result in a great deal of adult frustration!). Instead, give children creative materials and let each one work at an individual level. Engage children in conversation about the process of what they are doing. "Tell me about your picture." "I see lots of dots on your page. What color are your dots?" "Which kind of dough is softer? Which one do you like best?" Talk about colors and shapes you see, what the child seems to be enjoying, etc. Especially in a class of mixed ages, don't focus on activities where a finished product is the goal. This avoids comparison (older ones have already heard this kind of thing from even older children) and eliminates frustration.

Many early childhood activities can be stretched to fit different ability levels. For example, if making a collage of magazine pictures, a two-year-old may have finished after gluing two or three pictures, a three-year-old may want to cover the entire paper, a four-year-old may want to trim the pictures before gluing and a five-year-old may want to dictate captions for each picture. Wise teachers of mixed ages will choose activities that will provide each age level with successful participation.

During Bible story time, having at least one teacher and one helper for each group makes it possible to schedule two story times. Even better, keeping the story time as an activity center through which groups rotate makes it possible to tailor the story to each particular group. This way, all children are taught the Bible story on their own level. If this is not possible, use older children as part of the story-telling team. Invite them to answer questions and tell details that they want to share from the story. This not only gives older ones a sense of helpfulness and importance, but it also gives the teacher a chance to gauge what children do or do not understand about the story.

As with any other adjustment, ask for God's wisdom in the situation. Look for creative ways to see the matter of age span as a benefit, instead of a problem. Your attitude of accepting things as they are and your relaxed calmness will help each child sense God's love for him or her. As each one works at his or her own level, all ears will be open to the words you say about God and His care.

Music: Making Music Memorable

In today's world, music is often thought of as something to listen to, instead of something to make! Many adults claim they cannot sing, but especially in an early childhood classroom, every adult has absolute permission to cut loose and sing! Your singing teaches children that music is God's gift, that it brings joy and that it includes everyone. Beyond that, music is one of the most powerful teaching tools we have because of the combined impact of melody, rhythm and rhyme.

More Than a Solo Act

Sometimes a teacher is intimidated when a group of small children stare glassy-eyed while he or she sings a solo! Remember that children who have experienced music only as something to listen to will participate first by simply watching and listening. (The younger the child, the more listening and less singing he or she will do.) If a song doesn't include motions or clapping, add them. Clap on the rhythm or invent finger motions to go with it. When you do the motions, children can be involved as they imitate you, whether or not they are singing. One goal of music is to involve every child, so each one learns Scripture and biblical concepts in a fun and memorable way.

If you are deeply uncomfortable singing a song, repeat the words of the song as a poem or invite another member of your teaching team to lead the music. You may also play the music on a cassette or CD to help both you and children enjoy the music.

Remember, you are not performing or providing entertainment. You are using a song to guide children in learning. Your musical perfection is unimportant. However, your enthusiasm and interest are vital! Be willing to make mistakes. If you forget the tune, keep going with the words. Children will be delighted that you, too, are learning. Relax and enjoy the children's response to the songs. When you truly sing from a heart of love for the Lord, children are quick to catch your feeling of joy.

More Than a Time Filler

A song can fill in time gaps, regain children's attention or give them a chance to move. These are all good reasons to sing! However, avoid asking "What do you want to sing?" It takes some time for a child to make you understand what song he or she wants to sing, and the songs a child chooses are unlikely to relate to the lesson of the day.

Be sure to choose songs that reinforce the Bible truth for the day and contain biblical concepts that are clear to young children! Your curriculum should provide songs developed specifically to teach young children about God and to help them memorize Scripture in an age-appropriate way.

Some teachers may want to sing the old favorites. Too often, we adults have an emotional tie to a childhood song; however, our favorite childhood Sunday School songs may confuse young children! Consider first whether an old favorite will help children understand God's Word at their own level. Other teachers may feel most comfortable singing songs that they are used to singing in adult worship services. However, in most cases these songs use vocabulary and concepts that are abstract and symbolic in nature and, as a result, they are not understood by young children.

When you choose a song that reinforces the day's biblical truth, you are making the best use of every moment of teaching time. Give children as many chances as possible to learn biblical principles and Scripture while they sing, clap and have lots of fun!

More Than Voices

There are more ways to participate in music than simply singing! Besides involving every child through clapping and other motions, consider making some simple rhythm instruments. They will spice up any musical experience! Using rhythm instruments also develops a child's mind and coordination as well as being another way for a child to participate.

To Make Instruments

It doesn't require much money to make sturdy homemade rhythm instruments.

• Tie small bells together with sturdy string or ribbon for children to shake.

• Unsharpened pencils make excellent rhythm sticks or drumsticks.

• Drums come ready-made from empty coffee cans with plastic lids. Cover the can with colorful Con-Tact paper.

• A thrift-store pan lid makes a wonderful cymbal when struck with the eraser end of an unsharpened pencil.

• Shakers are easily made from plastic jars, small water bottles or salt boxes. Simply insert small stones, popcorn kernels, macaroni, beans or rice (each makes a different sound!); glue lid or opening securely closed. Children can then guess what item is inside making the sound. Shakers can be covered with colorful Con-Tact paper or decorated with puff paint or glitter.

To Use Instruments

Here are a few ideas of how to use the rhythm instruments in your class:

• Have a praise parade. Play a selected song from a children's cassette or CD while children march around the room, playing the instruments. Children may also simply play without a recording as they march.

• Play a freeze game. Play recorded music while children play instruments and walk in a circle. Stop the recorded music as a signal for children to freeze in place. After children freeze, they trade instruments with others and then continue again at your signal.

• Allow children to explore. At times, leave several instruments out with which children may experiment. You may wish to add a cassette player with a children's music tape already inserted. Children play the cassette and use the instruments to practice keeping time to the music.

Less of a Problem

Children may find ways to use the instruments that we adults haven't imagined! If a child uses an instrument as a weapon, simply take it and show the child the correct way to use it. Then invite the child to repeat your actions. "Bill, would you please show me how to use the sticks like I showed you?" Most children will need no further instruction.

Children may have difficulty sharing rhythm instruments. Be alert to reinforce their positive behavior. "Seth, I know you like the red shaker best. Thank you for giving Jake a turn with it, even when it's hard to do!"

Never tell a child to stop singing or to sing more quietly. When the noise level is too high, simply repeat the song in a whispery voice. "That was great! This time, let's sing the song in a whisper."

Enjoy children's freedom to make music with all they have. Singing with them can help you rediscover joy in your own voice!

Nature Center: Exploring God's World

A young child's plea "Let me see!" means "Let me touch, feel, shake, taste and smell it!" Nature Bible learning activities use the senses to heighten a child's ability to learn. Firsthand experiences are the core of learning for young children. Exploring God's world helps a child begin to sense the extent of God's love, care and wisdom. Hands-on exploring gives children many opportunities to learn about God and themselves. Whether taking a nature walk, touching items inside a bag or sniffing and comparing a series of scent containers, children are eager to explore their own abilities and the wonders of God's creation. Some nature Bible learning activities involve direct examination of natural items (bark, rocks, shells, leaves, etc.). Others involve the creation of scenes using natural materials such as sand, rocks and sticks, the collection and display of natural items or the discovery of the child's own wonderfully made characteristics.

Nature Bible learning activities may also incorporate those simple demonstrations of natural law that you may take for granted as an adult. Exploring the way magnets work or the way light makes a rainbow through a prism calls us back to sense the wonder of God's astounding plan and care. As we express our own wonder and appreciation, we truly and effectively communicate a great deal about God's character, love and power. A child will then sense that Bible truths are not separate from life but are a real part of it. Young children are natural learners full of curiosity and eager questions. Linking the truths of God's Word to the wonders of God's creation is delightfully easy!

Basic Materials

Having some basic materials on hand will enhance the experiences of the children and make it easy for you to lead children in hands-on examination of God's world. Include these items in your supplies: several magnifying glasses, a variety of nature items (rocks, shells, living plants, sticks, etc.), large tubs for water and/or shallow pans or boxes for sand play, fabrics in a variety of textures and newspaper or plastic tablecloths (to protect tabletops).

Guided Conversation

An essential part of the teacher's role in a nature Bible learning activity is to provide words for a child, helping him or her identify the experience and relate God to it. Once this relationship is made, the child is able to think about the Bible story or Bible verse in terms of a firsthand experience. Without such guidance, nature learning activities become just so many interesting experiences.

Some of the nature Bible learning activities will help familiarize children with a con-cept they will hear about in the Bible story. For example, pouring water through nail holes punched in an aluminum pie pan to simulate a rainstorm helps a child understand the big rainstorm in the story of Noah. Other nature Bible learning activities will encourage children to demonstrate obedience to a Bible verse as they experiment with items of God's wonderful creation.

Because they involve every part of the curious child, nature Bible learning activities will more than likely be a class favorite!

New Teacher: Help! I'm a New Teacher

When most of us were recruited as early childhood teachers, we thought the job mainly consisted of keeping little ones from hurting themselves or each other, providing snacks, singing songs and telling a Bible story. But as we teachers grow in understanding, just as our little ones grow in learning, we can see far more accomplished! Read the following guidelines for teaching young children. Remember, though, that your prayers for the children in your class are the best preparation of all!

What to Expect

• Young children learn by doing, not sitting. Play is their work. A fidgety class needs active ways to learn. Have several activities ready and let children choose where to begin. Discipline problems will decrease! Use the conversation ideas in every lesson to link the Bible truths to what you see children doing. "Hannah, I see you are drawing blue circles. God made your hands so that you could draw!"

• Young children have a very limited grasp of ideas that we as adults take for granted. They need for us to relate big biblical ideas (such as being kind or accepting God's love) to what they know or do. "Christie, you shared the dough with Josh. That is being kind!"

• A young child is not yet able to understand how his or her actions affect others. Guide the child toward desirable good behavior. "Seth! Hitting hurts! Until you remember not to hit, you cannot play with Justin. Right now you need to play with the blocks or look at books."

• Small children quickly absorb our attitudes! If you think a child is a problem, your attitude will show it. (And the child will probably become a bigger problem!) Pray for each child. Treat each one with the same kindness and respect you would show an adult.

What to Do

• Follow Jesus' example. Little children need far more action than talk. When Jesus was around little children, He loved them; He didn't lecture them. Actions say more than words ever could. Focus on the children. Listen to them. You are the living example of God's love to each little child!

• Get close. Put yourself at the child's eye level. Squat, kneel or sit. Before you talk, look into the child's eyes. You'll get the child's attention as well as send a message: "You're important to me. I care about you."

• Be positive. Tell a child what you want him or her to do, not what to STOP doing. "Marina, dough belongs on the table. Please pick it up off the floor. Thank you. You may use this cookie cutter."

• Be quick to see and point out what is good. "I see you sharing with Josiah, Kade. Being kind is a way to obey God's Word. Thank you." You've not only related the action to the Bible, but you've also helped both children better understand the concept of kindness!

• Give a child a choice. Even if a child is upset, giving a choice creates a new focus and puts responsibility for behavior back on the child. "Nathan, would you rather take turns with the blocks or glue pictures at the art table?" Whatever choices you offer, be sure that either choice is perfectly acceptable to you.

How to Prepare

• The job of preparation begins during the week prior to each class. Pray for yourself and the children in your class. For each lesson, read the Scripture for the lesson, even if it is a story with which you are familiar. Then in the teacher's guide read the summary of the lesson content and pay special attention to the goals of the lesson. Scan the overview chart to see the activities that are offered in the lesson and how each activity will help you meet the goals of the session. Choose the activities you will prepare and collect any needed materials.

• To prepare Bible learning activities, read the instructions for each activity to understand what the children will do to complete the activity. Think through how the activity will work in your space, with your materials and your children. Then become familiar with the suggested conversation which will help you connect children's actions to the lesson's Bible story or verse.

• To prepare for the telling of the Bible story, practice telling the story as written in the lesson so that you become familiar with the words and phrases appropriate for young children. As you tell the story, show the flannel figures (or other visual aids) to illustrate the story action, and keep your Bible open to the appropriate Scripture reference. Remind children that your words are from this special book of God's messages to us. State clearly that the stories in the Bible really happened.

• If a student activity page is provided with your curriculum, look at how it is to be completed and become familiar with the conversation suggestions. Teachers who are ready to talk with children about the Bible story and Bible verse make a big impact on the child's learning. Plan to complete your page in class as a demonstration for children so that children can work on their pages with a minimum of instruction from you.

Outside Play: The Great Outdoors

Children spend far more time indoors today than they did 50 years ago. Some adults see the outdoor world as a dangerous or inconvenient place; others contend that indoor activity is just as good. However, outdoor time is necessary for a young child's mental, physical and emotional development.

Valuable Experiences

Mentally, both thinking and coordination (muscle control) circuitry is laid into the brain largely before age five. Physically, the large muscles themselves need exercise to grow properly. Children who do not get enough large-muscle experience lack coordination. Emotionally, children who are indoors too long grow restless, irritable and distractible.

Few large-muscle activities can effectively take place in a classroom. When children need a mental or emotional break, the outdoors provides the change of scenery and change of pace they need. The senses are heightened and the child relaxes. When children are able to get outdoors, it can make a world of difference in their lives!

Something as simple as a nature walk can provide a wealth of experiences, no matter where you live. As you walk, compare shades of green in tree leaves, colors of flowers, heights and shapes of hills or rocks, smells of leaves. Compare textures of tree bark, stones or seeds. Take a sound walk, stopping often to close eyes and simply listen. Report the kinds of sounds you hear. Identify bird calls. Classify sounds as high, low, loud, quiet, etc. Ask questions. "What sounds do we hear that God made for us to enjoy?" "What things do we see that God made?" "What did God make that is green?"

Outdoor Games

Games for young children are not like organized sports with rules and times. Rather, they are planned ways to explore and experiment. When children are allowed to play outdoors, the ways to explore expand exponentially!

Sand Play

Playing in sand is such a basic outdoor activity for young children that it should never be neglected. To enrich sand play, provide a variety of plastic household items to expand children's imaginations: plastic ice-cube trays, plastic bottles with wide mouths, spray bottles of water, hula hoops, old paintbrushes and clean buckets, funnels and sifters or any other interesting items! Spray bottles provide water to wet sand and help to keep dust at a low level without soaking everyone in the sand play area.

Before children play in the sandbox, scan it for possible cat droppings and remove them. (A sandbox cover is a good investment!) When needed, remind children of a few simple sandbox rules: "We keep sand in the sandbox. We do not throw sand. We share sand toys."

As you remain nearby and observe children at play, you'll find many natural opportunities to connect children's actions to God's Word. "Evan, thank you for giving Ella a turn with the big truck. Sharing is a way to obey God."

After children play in the sand, use large scrub brushes to brush off shoes and clothes. Be sure children wash their hands as well.

Running

Running is a natural activity for children, and where better to run than outdoors? Make a short running course by setting out traffic cones or small chairs to mark a path. Invite children to show how many ways they can move along the path (hopping, tiptoeing, etc.). To increase the challenge, move cones apart and show children how to run in and out between the cones in a slalom pattern.

Throwing

Any throwing experience that can be done indoors is even better outdoors! Many more types of balls can be used outdoors. Besides tossing and rolling balls, invite children to practice moving the ball hand to hand or through the legs, or try bowling with empty two-liter bottles. Simple hockey-type play is easy to do with beach balls and long cardboard tubes or sheets of newspaper rolled together lengthwise. Scoop tosses for smaller balls are easily made from plastic gallon jugs with handles.

Climbing

Play equipment may or may not be part of your outdoor experience. But a sharp-eyed teacher can spot a tree suitable for young children to climb: smooth bark, low branches and good places to boost and hold on to. With two adults acting as spotters, it's easy to give children the thrill of climbing a tree! If a child is not ready to try climbing alone, simply lift the child into the crotch of the tree to enjoy the view.

Whatever ways you choose to use the outdoors, tie children's enjoyment to God's goodness with your words. "God loves you, Mia. He gave you strong legs to run and jump!" "Look at those birds in the tree. God makes sure they have food. God loves the birds. He loves you even more!"

Play Dough: Kids Love Learning with Play Dough

Dough play is one of the most valuable kinds of play young children can do! For a young child, the joy that comes from working with dough is the feeling of being in control of a substance. There is no way to do it wrong. Children can pound, roll, squeeze or shape dough any way they like.

Dough play is another place where process, not product, is the watchword. A wise adult remains nearby to watch, to interact with the children and to enjoy each child's process of creativity and discovery. A finished product is usually not at all important to the young child. It should not be overly important to the adult, either! Many teachers, especially those of younger children, provide play dough each week as an activity in which children may participate.

Tools and Rules

Give each child a fist-sized lump of dough. To enrich dough play, provide toy rolling pins, short lengths of dowel, craft sticks or plastic knives to flatten and cut dough. Seasonal cookie cutters can be an occasional addition, but it's usually best for children to make shapes of their own choosing.

As children work with dough, roll and play with the dough yourself, but avoid making representational items. This is a tough temptation for some of us; the artistically inclined have the urge to shape a cat and say, "Look! I made a cat." However, you have now created a model that some children will feel that they must copy in order to be acceptable. This makes the child dis-

satisfied with what he or she has made and uncertain about his or her own abilities. Make it your goal to help the children feel successful in what they can do themselves, not how well they can imitate an adult-made model.

One comment all children should hear often about any art or dough activity is "It's OK to make your art look any way you want it to be."

There are only three rules that apply to dough play: "We keep the dough on the table. We keep the dough out of our mouths. We share the dough and the equipment."

Before and After

To make dough play easy to clean up, make a few simple preparations. Lay an old sheet (attach Velcro strips to undersides of the corners to keep it secure) or a large flannel-backed vinyl tablecloth under the dough table. (Newspapers still work in a pinch!) Provide a plastic place mat, sheet of waxed paper or a paper plate at each child's place. When it's time to clean up, invite children to take a small ball of dough and play "magnet," pressing the ball on small dough crumbs until they cannot see any more crumbs. This is a fun and effective way to get the majority of the table clean! Paper towels, premoistened towelettes or a no-rinse hand-wiping solution makes cleaning hands and table simple and easy. Store play dough in airtight containers and make a fresh batch after several uses.

Prayer: Young Children Talk to God

Prayer can be a meaningful part of worship for young children. However, it is sometimes done in ways that make it seem strange, boring and unrelated to a child's life. What are some ways we can help young children grow in their desire and ability to express themselves to God?

Understanding in Words

As much of a mystery as prayer is to some of us adults, what can young children understand about prayer?

• God wants us to talk to Him. He wants to hear what we have to say!

• We can pray anytime—not only in Sunday School or church but in the car, at the store, anywhere!

• We can pray by saying words out loud or by saying words to ourselves. We can sing prayers, too.

• We close our eyes because it helps us think about what we are talking to God about, instead of what we see around us.

Understanding in Action

The way you pray teaches far more about prayer than any words you say! When you pray, it shows children that prayer is important to you. Your attitude of reverence and trust is keenly felt by a child. When you pray, you show children what prayer is. If your prayers are short and specific and if they make sense to a young child, you are also teaching that prayer is simple, genuine and deals with things that matter to young children.

If you think that prayer is mainly for grown-ups or that young children aren't yet able to pray, your prayers will reflect it. Because young children so easily absorb unspoken adult attitudes, they will soon conclude that they can't pray. Instead, take this opportunity to consider what Jesus said about our need to become like little children! Prayer is not a performance for God or for anyone else. Enjoy learning how to pray simply, honestly and directly. It will change your prayer life and will effectively teach prayer to children.

Throughout a class session, provide opportunities for short, simple prayers during activities. "Look at the way your hands can draw those little circles, Josh! Let's thank God for your hands. Dear God, thank You for Josh's hands. They can draw little circles! In Jesus' name, amen." "Jenna, you shared the crayons with Eliot. That's a way to obey God's Word. Thank You, God, that Jenna knows how to share. In Jesus' name, amen." These occasional and natural prayers teach a child that God cares about every part of life.

If a child is reluctant to pray or unfamiliar with praying aloud, involve the child in prayer in other ways. For example, ask a question. "What is something you like to eat?" Then include the child's answer in a thank-you prayer. "What is one way to obey God by being kind?" After the child answers, ask God's help in being kind, mentioning the specific way suggested by the child.

To help children know prayers need not always be spoken, sing songs that are prayers with the children. Comment, "The words of the song are meant to be sung to God. It is a prayer." Children may wish to close their eyes as they sing, to help them remember that the song is a prayer.

Understanding Bible Prayers

Adults may feel that young children should memorize Scripture prayers such as the Lord's Prayer or a prayer from the Psalms. While it is true that young children have a facility for memorization and that words memorized in early childhood are well-remembered, these Scriptural phrases are long and many of the words are beyond a young child's understanding. When a child is older, memorizing these significant passages will be a more meaningful experience than during early childhood.

Remember, the most meaningful and trustworthy way to teach children about prayer is your prayers. Ask God to work by His Spirit to use your example—and trust Him to do so, in childlike faith!

Recipes: Art Recipes You Can Use!

Providing a variety of art materials for the children you teach is easier (and cheaper!) than you think—as you'll discover with these recipes. It is always best to make a sample of the recipe ahead of time, adjusting the amounts for the number of children in your class. If you teach children who are likely to put things in their mouths, only use recipes that are made with food items. Store all mixtures in airtight containers.

Cornstarch Paint

3 teaspoons cornstarch
2 teaspoons white vinegar
Food coloring

Mix corn starch and vinegar. Add food coloring to achieve desired color. Paint is smooth.

Corn Syrup Paint

1 teaspoon corn syrup
1 tablespoon liquid tempera paint

Mix corn syrup and tempera paint. When dry, paint will be shiny.

Cream-Cheese Play Dough

8-ounce package of cream cheese, softened
1/2 cup nonfat dry milk
1 tablespoon honey
1/2 cup flour

Combine cream cheese, milk and honey in a bowl and mix until well blended. Add approximately 1/2 cup flour to make dough workable. Children form shapes. (Optional: Place shapes on crackers for a snack.) Keep dough refrigerated. Discard dough on expiration date shown on cream cheese package.

Face Paint

3 tablespoons Crisco shortening

2 tablespoons cornstarch
Food coloring

Mix shortening and cornstarch. Add food coloring to achieve desired color. Apply paint with fingers or small paintbrush with stiff bristles. Wash off paint with soap and water.

Finger Paint

1 cup flour
1 cup water
1 1/2 teaspoons salt
Food coloring

Mix flour, water and salt. Add food coloring to achieve desired color.

Kool-Aid Paint

Unsweetened Kool-Aid packet(s)
1/4 cup glue

Mix one or more Kool-Aid packets into glue. Makes a thick, bright paint. Will also work as face paint. Paint can be thinned by adding water. Children paint with paintbrushes. When dry, the paint will be glossy.

Make-Your-Own Stickers

2 tablespoons boiling water
1 tablespoon Jell-O

Mix two tablespoons of boiling water with one tablespoon of any flavor Jell-O. Paint mixture to back of paper shapes or small pictures children have drawn. Set aside to dry. Children lick stickers.

Pud

1/2 box cornstarch
Water

Pour cornstarch onto shallow cookie tray. Add water slowly and

stir until mixture thickens. Children use their hands to play with the mixture.

Puff Paint

1/3 cup glue

2/3 cup shaving cream

Mix glue with shaving cream. Mixture will puff up. (Optional: Add food coloring.) Children paint with craft sticks. (Note: Using equal parts of glue and shaving cream makes a finger paint.)

Rock Salt Goo

1 cup white glue

1 cup rock salt

6 to 8 drops food coloring

Mix rock salt and food coloring. Add glue and mix for several minutes. Children will enjoy using hands to play with the goo!

Salt and Flour Play Dough

2 parts flour

1 part salt

1 tablespoon alum for every 2 cups flour

Food coloring

1 part water

Mix dry ingredients well. Add food coloring to water to achieve desired color. Slowly pour colored water into dry ingredients; mix and add water until dough forms a ball around spoon. Knead dough on floured board. If dough is sticky, add more flour. If dough is too stiff, slowly add more water.

Salt, Flour and Cornstarch Play Dough

1 1/2 cups flour

1 cup cornstarch

1 cup salt

Food coloring

1 1/4 cups warm water

Mix dry ingredients. Add food coloring to warm water. Slowly pour and mix colored water into dry ingredients until dough forms a ball around spoon. Knead dough on floured board. If dough is sticky, add more flour. If dough is too stiff, slowly add more water.

Sand Dough

1 cup sand

1/2 cup cornstarch

1 teaspoon granulated alum

3/4 cup hot water

Mix dry ingredients in pot. Add hot water and stir vigorously. Cook over medium heat until thick, stirring constantly. Remove from pot and let cool. Knead dough for 20 to 30 seconds.

Sawdust Dough

2 1/2 cups sawdust or commercially purchased wood shavings

1 cup flour

1 cup salt

1 cup water

Mix dry ingredients well. Add water a little at a time, stirring until mixture reaches a stiff but pliable consistency. Add more flour and water if dough is too crumbly. Knead dough until it becomes elastic.

Shampoo Paint

3 teaspoons shampoo

Small amount of water

Food coloring

Stir shampoo, water and food coloring until frothy.

Sidewalk Paint

1/4 cup cornstarch

1/4 cup water

Food coloring

Mix cornstarch and water together. Stir in six to eight drops of food coloring. (Use additional food coloring for a more intense color.) As they paint, children dip brushes frequently into the paint. Paint will wash off with water.

Watercolor Paint

Kool-Aid packet

2 teaspoons water

Mix Kool-Aid with water. Paint will smell fragrant.

Relationships: Benefits of Building Relationships

When we adults are focused on the details of getting through a class session, it can be easy to forget that no matter how good our activities or how important our point, nothing transforms a life more effectively than building a relationship. In fact, relationship is the very reason Christ died and rose—that we might live in relationship, first with God the Father through Him and then with each other by the power of His Spirit! Relationship is the essence of God's Kingdom.

Three Reasons to Care

• On any given day, a child who enters your classroom may be under tremendous stress. Even a young child may be dealing with situations such as a recent move, a new baby-sitter, death of a pet, lack of food or shelter, divorce or even child abuse. Attention from parents may be limited. We never know where a child has been emotionally and spiritually.

It is imperative that *every* child be given loving acceptance, hugs, smiles and genuine interest! Often the child with the most negative behavior is the one who needs the greatest measure of loving acceptance and positive interest.

• School settings generally cannot make up for a lack of relationship at home. Most teachers are overburdened and must focus on the group, rather than individual children. But we have the opportunity to minister to young children simply through

seeing each one as a real person made in God's image. As we use each child's name, as we touch, talk and encourage each one as a person worthy of our respect and love, children absorb information about what God's love looks like, sounds like and feels like.

• Coming from different neighborhoods, children in a class may not know each other well. We can minister to them by gently helping them learn how to build relationships with other children in a safe, loving environment where relationship is valued highly. Children need to know that at church, people love them and love each other. These are people whom they can love freely and safely. There is no better place to begin building unity in the Body of Christ than here!

Three Benefits of Caring

• We are giving the child a model to imitate. Paul instructed in 1 Corinthians 11:1, "Follow my example, as I follow the example of Christ." Our job is to show, rather than tell, what it means to live as a follower of Jesus. As we are transparent with children, they will get to know us. They will begin to unconsciously identify with and imitate Christlike character, beliefs and values. Our smiles, our touches, our hugs and our gracious reactions to surprising situations teach more effectively what it means to live as a Christian than even good curriculum or excellent activities.

• As we help children get to know and appreciate each other, we are also leading them to experience the Church, the Body of Christ. Children have the chance to know firsthand that believers in Jesus live and work together as a team, living in sympathy and harmony, instead of competition.

• We benefit by getting to know young children! Not only do we become better teachers by understanding their needs and feelings, but we also have the delightful privilege of seeing the world through their fresh and unspoiled eyes! We often gain surprising insights that help us better understand Christ's desire that we come to His kingdom as little children.

Three Ways to Show You Care

Make it a rule in your classroom that these three behaviors welcome every child:

• Conversation and attention to what the child says at his or her eye level

• A kind touch on the shoulder

• A genuine smile that says, "I'm glad to see you today!"

The job of welcoming children should be assigned to the same helper or teacher each week so that children who have difficulty separating from their parents will have the opportunity to build a relationship with a friendly adult. Don't leave this important job unassigned. When children feel welcomed and are given a choice of activities as they enter, they will play and work together better and will more easily learn to obey God's Word in real, practical ways!

Salvation: Guiding the Young Child Toward Jesus

Each of us moves through the spiritual development of life in as much of an individual rate and way as we do in any other area. God knows each person intimately; therefore, He works differently in every life. Whatever one's rate of growth or plan of development, God is tirelessly at work to bring us into closer relationship with Himself! Acknowledging this helps us rest in His good plan and look for His hand in the experiences that cause us and our children to develop spiritually.

When we present Jesus consistently by both our actions and our words, we lay a foundation for a child to receive Christ as Savior. When is a child ready to receive Christ? Remembering God's ceaseless work, we need to be sensitive facilitators of that process. God's Holy Spirit calls a child into relationship in His time, not ours. We should never put up walls, but we also should never push or manipulate children. We need to give children time and opportunity to ask questions, think through ideas and respond at their own pace. While some children at this age level (especially from Christian homes) may indeed pray to become members of God's family, accepting Jesus as their Savior, expect wide variation in children's readiness for this important step.

• To help a child give words to thoughts and feelings about Jesus, ask many open-ended what-do-you-think and tell-me-more questions. "Tell me what you like best about Jesus" will help you gain insight into what a child does or does not understand. This will also help you to give a child the information he or she needs, instead of an answer that does not apply! Kindergartners especially want to know more about many aspects of God. Every question we answer creates an opportunity to help the child understand more about a personal relationship with Jesus.

• Talk individually with children. Something as important as a child's personal relationship with Jesus Christ can be handled more effectively alone than in a group.

• Talk simply. Phrases such as "born again" or "Jesus in my heart" are symbolic and far beyond a young child's understanding. Focus on how God makes people a part of His family.

Consistently share this information whenever a child seems interested but only for as long as the interest lasts. Lay a good foundation for a lifetime of solid spiritual growth!

Talking About Salvation

God loves us, but we have done wrong things (sinned).

God says sin must be punished.

God sent Jesus to take the punishment for the wrong things we have done.

*We can tell God that we have done wrong and tell Him we are sorry for our sin.
    We can ask Jesus to be our Savior.*

Then God forgives us and we become a part of God's family.

Schedule: Guidelines for Making Your Class Schedule Work

For maximum learning in early childhood classes, a schedule creates a few firm points that allow for a great deal of flexibility in between!

Preparation

We are far more successful in every aspect of teaching if we are well prepared. The teacher's early arrival allows time to lay out materials, plan for a variety of factors unique to that day and pray with other teachers or helpers.

(Note: If children will be in a session either before or after Sunday School, plan carefully what children will be doing during the transition time between sessions, which staff will be responsible for supervising children and how arrival and departure of children will be handled with a minimum of disruption to the ongoing program.)

Bible Learning Activities

Teaching begins when the first child arrives! Teachers should never be busy with preparation when even the earliest arrival comes to the classroom door. One adult should be

Schedule

Step 1
Bible Learning Activities 20-30 minutes

Purpose: To help children talk about and practice Bible truths while participating in one or more learning activities.

Step 2
Bible Story Time 10-15 minutes

Purpose: To provide children with informal worship opportunities and to help children hear and respond to a Bible story and Bible verse.

Step 3
Bible Sharing Time 15 minutes

Purpose: To help children review the Bible story and talk about ways to obey the Bible verse in everyday life.

ready to greet each child and offer a choice of activities. The teacher's readiness ensures that children are not left to wander about the classroom and that valuable teaching time is not wasted. Greet each child at his or her eye level; listen to what the child has to tell. Help the child become involved in an activity. Teachers and helpers should be ready at each activity to guide conversation that helps children understand the day's lesson focus as well as give children ideas of how to expand an activity.

Why begin with Bible learning activities? Why not begin with an assembly? An organized assembly or circle time is very difficult to begin with the first child's arrival, and each subsequent arrival is distracting. Waiting to begin wastes the best part of the schedule. At the last meeting you attended, when were you most interested and alert? Probably at the beginning! If you had to wait for everyone to arrive so that the meeting could begin, your interest probably lagged. Preschoolers are "here and now" people. While they are fresh and eager to learn, they need immediate involvement in activities that will connect God's Word to their lives. Beginning with an assembly time also often creates greater separation problems. A shy or reluctant

child finds it easier to become involved in a fun and inviting learning activity.

Ideally, there should be two or more Bible learning activities ready as children arrive, so children are able to choose which activity they prefer to participate in first. A teacher or helper should be in each area, ready to involve children and engage them in conversation. To effectively involve a child in an activity, begin to do it yourself. As children become involved, remain nearby to observe, engage in conversation and relate the children's activities to the lesson focus and Bible verse for the session.

If one learning activity area overflows with children, teachers in the other areas should invite children to join them. If the overflow persists (some activities are simply a big hit!), rotate children through that activity, so everyone has a turn; use colors of clothing, type of shoe, etc. as simple ways of dividing the group.

Near the end of Bible Learning Activity Time, it's important to let children know what is coming next. Go to each area and tell children it will soon be time to clean up. Signal the beginning of cleanup time with a song or chant, so everyone can join in the song or chant as they begin. One teacher should move to the Bible Story

Time area so that the first children who arrive there don't have to wait but can begin an involving activity. This also encourages others to finish cleanup and come to the Bible Story Time area.

Bible Story Time

The second major time segment in the schedule brings all the children and teachers together in a semicircle on the floor. (Children may sit in chairs or on carpet squares if the floor is not carpeted.) Bible Story Time is made up of several components: a gathering activity to help children readily join the large group, a song or two, a prayer, an interactive activity that involves repetition of the Bible verse and the Bible story.

The variety of experiences in Bible Story Time helps children experience a needed change of pace in the session. Children will tire less readily when they are given a balance of active and quiet things to do. This time spent in a large group also helps the teacher call attention to the lesson focus as each activity takes place.

Telling the Bible story is a key component

of the large-group time. The objective in telling Bible stories to young children is not primarily for them to remember the details of the events; it is to allow the narrative to reveal God's involvement in everyday life. Introduce the Bible story by asking a question, giving a listening task or showing a story-related household item that will catch children's attention. Use the flannel figures or other visual aids provided to illustrate story action. Conclude the story by linking the action of the main character to the lives of the children.

Some churches prefer to divide the class into groups of four to six children with a teacher telling the story to each small group. In these small groups there is ample opportunity for personal interaction between teacher and children.

At the end of Bible Story Time, briefly give directions for the next time segment. Dismiss children a few at a time (dismiss according to what color children are wearing, first letters of first names, with a song, etc.) to tables to complete their activity pages. This way, there is not a stampede but an orderly movement to the next part of the schedule.

Bible Sharing Time

During Bible Sharing Time, teachers lead children in completing an activity page. The activity page is a personalized visual aid for each child to use in reviewing the Bible story and in sharing together ways the Bible truth can be applied in everyday life. Be ready to use your activity page to demonstrate how to complete the page. Your visual example of the steps needed will do more to help children understand what to do than all your words combined!

As children complete the activity page, talk with them about the Bible story. Use the questions suggested on the page and in your teacher's guide. Invite children to use their completed pages to tell you the story.

Transition

When children have finished their activity pages, be sure to plan what they will do next. Some churches dismiss children to a free time of outdoor or indoor play, providing children with a much needed change of pace. Other churches continue with valuable teaching, making use of the enrichment activities provided in their teacher's guides. Continuing on with enrichment activities help parents get a glimpse of the kind of learning in which children have participated. Activities continue until parents (or the next session's staff) arrive.

Take a moment at the end of every class session to ask yourself and your coworkers, "Did the children accomplish the aims listed in the curriculum? Why or why not?" As you take a few minutes to review, you'll find strategies that work best for your class, successes with which to encourage each other and matters for prayer throughout the week.

Separation Anxiety: Helping Parents and Children Say Good-Bye

When some young children (especially in a class with two- and/or three-year-olds) enter a classroom and leave their parents behind for the first few times, chaos can ensue! What are some ways to make separation easier?

Allow Time and Acknowledge Feelings

Always remember (and gently remind parents) that when a child cries at separation time, it is not necessarily a problem. Young children *should* prefer their parents to a stranger! A child needs time to become familiar with you and the other adults in the class. This adjustment period is usually fairly brief, especially if teachers and helpers commit to teaching every week. Your calm reassurance of both parents and child will make the separation easier all around.

Say words that show you understand. "I know you are having a hard time. I know you'll miss your daddy. I know it's hard when your daddy leaves. He will be back soon." Help a child know that you recognize and accept his or her feelings.

Know that every child handles transitions differently. Some will cry again when it's time to leave! If a child is under stress (a parent is ill, parents are separated, a parent is gone a lot, etc.), he or she is more likely to be clingy and afraid. A child's anxiety may return from time to time. Just when a child seems comfortable with separation, he or she may revert back into anxiety. This is not a failure on anyone's part but simply a normal part of growth that is best dealt with calmly.

Establish a welcoming routine. Sing the same welcoming song every week, repeat the same poem or tell the child interesting things you'll be doing in class. Encourage a parent to tell the child that he or she will return: "I'll be back after you've played with toys and listened to a story." Then be ready to involve the child in an interesting activity. With a routine, children know what to expect, and separation should become easier.

Try These Tips

• The same person should greet an anxious child each time and involve him or her in an activity.

• Talk calmly to the child, even if he or she is crying loudly. Your gentle, soothing voice will help the child begin to relax. Communicate calmness and comfort by your words, voice and body posture. A young child will then be likely to relax as well! Singing softly to a young child is also very relaxing.

• For some children, too much contact too soon with a stranger results in more fear. Take time to talk further with the parent, so the child sees that the parent trusts and accepts you. If a child is obviously frigh-

tened by your attention, use indirect interaction. Begin an activity. Talk about what you are doing. As the child becomes involved, talk directly to the child.

• If the anxiety is severe, invite a parent to stay for a while, instead of coming back to check on a child repeatedly. (Checking back can amount to four or five good-byes, upsetting the child each time the parent leaves!) When a parent stays, try having him or her leave for five minutes and then come back for the remainder of the session. Over several sessions, increase the length of each absence until the child and parent are comfortable with separation.

• Send a picture of the teachers home with the child or visit the family to increase familiarity. Remind parents that when they bring their child each week, repetition and familiarity help to keep separation from becoming a weekly problem. Tell parents about a specific activity or other child the child seemed to enjoy. Encourage parents to talk with the child about coming to "build with the big blocks" or "play with your friend Madeline," rather than just "coming to church."

Sharing: What Can Children Learn About Sharing?

We allow our expectations for each child to vary according to our understanding of his or her unique developmental pace. But when it comes to sharing, grown-ups may hold expectations that are less realistic! To adults, taking turns, or sharing, means cooperation and equal participation. But it has a far different meaning to a child. To young children, taking turns means one child has to give up something, with the possibility of being left with nothing in its place. To the child, it doesn't seem fair! Yet sharing is important and necessary for children to learn as they grow and mature.

Characteristics

Expect that younger preschoolers will not understand much of what it means to share or ways to share. Two-year-olds are discovering the boundaries between themselves and others. "NO!" and MINE!" help describe those boundaries—and others'

rights are not yet understood! Since twos are often involved in parallel play (alongside others but not with them), conflicts may be fierce but less common. Three-year-olds are more likely to interact in play with others and "M-I-I-INE!" is still a familiar cry. When conflict arises with younger preschoolers, it's usually more effective to distract them than to talk too much. For instance, as Mia grabs Joe's ball, describe what you see: "Mia, I see you want the blue ball." Describe a solution: "It is Joe's turn with the blue ball. Here is another ball for you to play with." If you promise a turn with the blue ball later, be sure to keep your word!

Four- and five-year-olds are growing in social awareness. They also have more of a desire to please others and have grown both in their ability to wait and in their understanding that taking a turn means you get to keep it—but only for a while. Acknowledge and encourage children's

actions of sharing. "Darla, you shared the block with Brandon. Thank you! That is a way to be kind, as our Bible says to do."

Ideas into Actions

Because taking turns, being kind and sharing are not concrete ideas, they are not grasped in a single class session or through a single lecture.

First, sharing must be demonstrated—by us. Describe ways to share as you demonstrate them. "Liam, I am cutting the apple into slices so that we can all share. Here is one slice for you and one slice for Ethan." When we model kindness and sharing, children see it as well as hear it. They learn far more than when we use words alone! For real learning to take place, examples and experiences must be repeated. Describe these experiences aloud to give children more ways to gain understanding.

To some children, taking turns will still feel like losing out. Because of a child's natural self-centeredness and short memory, it may seem to them that their turn never comes! When you intervene in a dispute, point out times when you have seen a child receive kind actions of others. "Nicki, Meg gave you first turn with the doll. She shared with you. You are sharing with her now. It is her turn. There will still be time for you to have another turn." After Meg has finished with the doll, say, "Nicki, Meg had her turn. Now it is your turn."

As you watch children peacefully involved in an activity together, don't assume that you are not needed! Watch carefully and give suggestions to help children think of ways to share. "Bill, Heidi needs a truck. You have lots of trucks. What could you do to help Heidi?" Keep comments and suggestions brief; children's attention spans are short!

In an art activity, provide two or three of items such as scissors and glue bottles to be shared by four to six children. Large-scale art activities such as murals and collages help children learn to work side by side. While each child's contribution will be unique, the child will enjoy feeling part of a group effort.

Block and dramatic play activities also provide children with opportunities to practice sharing. Children will enjoy taking turns to stack blocks for a tower. The shared task of building a road will also help children learn to make decisions about how they will work together. In dramatic play, encourage activities such as cleaning house or preparing a pretend meal. Such tasks enable children to have fun while learning ways to help each other.

Expect that a child's willingness to share will vary from week to week. This is a normal part of development. Solve problems in a matter-of-fact manner. "Mara, it's time to give Leia a turn. Maybe next week it will be easier for you to share. Giving a turn is a way to share, like our Bible tells us to do." Simply state the Bible principle; don't force the child.

Skills: Helping Children Fold, Tape, Cut and Glue

To help children successfully complete some of the activities suggested in your curriculum, a few basic skills are required. These skills—folding, taping, cutting and gluing—must be learned. And as you know, not all children learn at the same rate. Read these suggestions for a variety of ways to help children learn to succeed at these four tasks.

Folding

1. Before giving paper to a child, prefold paper as needed and then open it back up. Paper will then fold easily along the pre-folded lines when child refolds it.

2. Score the line to be folded by placing a ruler on the line. Then press firmly with a used ballpoint pen with no ink in it along the ruler's edge. The line will fold easily into place.

3. Hold the corners of the paper in position to be folded. Tell the child to press and rub where he or she wants to fold the page.

Taping

1. An easy solution for the problems of taping is to use double-sided tape whenever appropriate. Lay the tape down on the paper where it is needed. Child attaches the item that needs to be taped.

2. If double-sided tape is not available or is not appropriate, place a piece of tape lightly on the page where indicated. Child rubs on tape to attach it securely to paper.

Cutting

1. Cutting with scissors is one of the most difficult tasks for any young child to master. Provide scissors that are the appropriate size for young children and designed for both right-handed and left-handed children. (Purchase at educational supply stores.) All scissors should be approximately 4 inches (10 cm) long and should have blunt ends.

2. Hold paper tightly at ends or sides while child cuts.

3. Begin to cut paper for child to follow. Child follows cut you have begun.

4. Draw simple lines outside actual cut lines for the child to follow. This will help a child cut close to the desired shape—though it will not be exact.

5. Provide scrap paper for child to practice cutting.

Gluing

1. Have child use a glue bottle to apply a spot of glue to a large sheet of paper; then child presses a smaller piece of paper onto glued area.

2. Provide a glue stick for the child to use (available at variety stores). Take off cap and roll up a short amount of the glue stick for child. Child "colors" with glue stick over desired area.

3. Pour glue into a shallow container. Thin slightly by adding a small amount of water. Child uses paintbrush to spread glue over desired area. This idea works well when a large surface needs to be glued.

4. To glue a smaller surface, pour a small amount of glue into a shallow container. Give each child a cotton swab. Child dips the swab into the glue and rubs on desired area.

5. When using glue bottles, buy the smallest bottles for children to use. Refill small bottles from a large bottle. Adjust top to limit amount of glue that comes out. Instruct child to put "tiny dots of glue" on paper. Clean off and tightly close top of bottle when finished. Have several paper towels ready to clean up any spills or excess glue.

Remember not to expect perfection. Accept all attempts at accomplishing the task. Specific and honest praise will encourage the child to attempt the task again!

Snack Center: Food in the Classroom

Little children need to eat often! But more than providing nutrition or a way to stay occupied, snack times can become a time of social and spiritual benefit as well. At any age, in any culture, eating together comforts and unifies people. We can make a snack time a part of the day's teaching, instead of an incidental time-filler.

Regular Snack Times

If snack time is a regular feature of your class, give it importance. Use a transition signal (such as a song or finger play) to tell children it is time to wash hands and sit down. (If washing facilities are not available, be sure children clean hands with premoistened towelettes, a no-rinse hand-wiping solution or paper towels.)

Seat everyone. Space teachers and helpers around the table for easy conversation with children. Teachers and helpers should not hover over children. Serve snack items from trays—one tray per teacher and group. Involve children in helping by handing out napkins, cups, etc.

Be sure to pray or invite volunteers to pray. Genuinely and simply thank God for the food. Talk about where the food comes from or about the color or taste. Your appreciation for what God has given will be contagious!

As teachers are with children, they can encourage friendly conversation, and then let children take the lead. As they see children share, take turns, etc., they are there to acknowledge and encourage those actions. "Erika, I see you gave Chad a napkin. Thank you. That is a way to be kind. The Bible says to be kind."

Snack Center Tips

When children prepare a snack as a learning activity, they have the chance to practice many skills, from measuring and mixing to learning to work together in new ways.

A teacher or helper should always be present at the snack center. Most children have hearty appetites for snack food! At the snack center, involve children in estimating how much is needed so that each person in the group shares equally.

Some children may not want to leave the snack center. If a child has finished his or her helping, invite the child to help clean up or play out some other aspect of mealtime in the dramatic play area.

Food Concerns

Food for snacks should be nutritious. It may be easy to distribute candy or open a box of cookies, but there are many alternatives that will satisfy children. Try fruit slices, baby carrots, celery with cream cheese, small cups of yogurt with granola topping or cheese cubes.

There are many foods that are not recommended for young children, such as popcorn, peanuts and other nuts, chocolate and peanut butter. Some of these are a choking hazard and some cause such severe allergic reactions in a few children that they are literally deadly. Because some children have food allergies, it's important to post information for parents any time you are using food in class. Post this information where parents will see it at check-in time, so they can discuss any allergies with you. Also check children's registration cards for food allergies.

Some churches have color-coded dots on children's ID badges as food-allergy alerts. When visitors come, give parents a blank adhesive name badge on which they may note any allergies.

Storytelling: Tell Me a Story!

In the world of fast-paced entertainment, hi-tech effects and outrageous animation, children still love the eye-to-eye, person-to-person wonder of a good story well-told! It doesn't take a special gift to tell a good story, only a few developed skills. Good story times are warm and inviting. Children should be able to see you and any visual aids easily.

Prepare and Practice: If you don't know the details of the story, you won't tell them! Be sure to read the story until you are familiar with it. If you are nervous about using gestures or maintaining good eye contact, practice in front of a mirror to help you see what does and does not work within the story.

Capture Interest: Use an object or a question that catches children's interest to "hook" their attention. Don't tell too much in the introduction. Tantalize your audience!

Keep to the Main Idea: Read the lesson aims to find out what the main idea of the story is. For young children, one main point is enough. End with the main idea to help everyone identify the Bible truth.

Vary Your Voice: Talk louder, softer, faster or slower to emphasize dramatic points and keep interest high. (Don't be afraid to talk a little more slowly at times. It gives young children needed time to imagine the scene or action you are describing.)

Express with Your Face and Hands: Practice expressions and gestures while keeping good eye contact. Also practice pantomime motions and using your hands to make sound effects. Children focused on your face and hands are likely to pay good attention!

Prepare Visual Aids: If you are using visual aids (flannel figures, pictures, puppets, household objects, etc.), be sure to practice using them. Prepare and place them so that you can keep good eye contact with your audience during use. Remember that the best storytelling keeps props simple so that children's imaginations are stimulated to the maximum!

Tell It Again: Young children love to hear the same story over and over again, so once you have a story well in hand, know that your "performance" won't be a one-time thing! Look for opportunities during activities to tell or retell the story. "Nathan, what you just did is like someone in our Bible story. The Bible tells us that . . ." You may need to condense the story in this situation.

The objective of telling a Bible story is to make a Bible truth come alive to children. Restate the main idea and help children understand how it applies to their lives. (This is done for you in the teacher's guide version of the story.) When you have done that, stop! Give children a moment to absorb the point.

As with any other skill, you will find that the more stories you tell, the better you can do it! Don't stop to worry about what the children will think. They are the least critical and most appreciative audience in the world!

Take-Home Papers: Getting the Message Home!

After any given church service, parents leave with a gaggle of children on one hand and a fistful of papers in the other. Art projects, activity pages, take-home papers, bulletins and notices—a profusion of paper that can leave us in confusion! Could this be one reason these papers too often end up either in the parking lot or on the floor of the car? When we understand the purpose for using these papers at home effectively, they can extend and expand a child's classroom learning. The *FamilyTime* take-home paper was designed to help your child learn about God all week long in a variety of ways. To use this paper to enrich your child's understanding, try these page-by-page tips:

• **Page 1** tells you immediately what Bible content your child covered in class. The picture has two questions with it. Ask your child either or both questions as you show the picture.

The lesson's Bible verse is listed, along with two questions to help your child think about the meaning of the verse.

The statement below those questions is the day's lesson focus (the point of the lesson, already made in class in several ways).

• **Pages 2 and 3** are designed to provide enjoyable interaction with your child all week long. Read the interactive story several times during the week at bedtime or story time. Young children love repetition and learn best through hearing a story over and over.

The simple parent-and-child activity listed under FamilyTalk can be enjoyed anytime. This activity uses questions to help you and your child talk about a common household item in a way that can help to review the Bible story. PrayerTime contains questions and a prayer to help you and your child learn to pray together in an age-appropriate way.

• **Page 4** contains articles that are just for you! These articles provide ideas for you to consider both as a person and a parent. They also share ways to help you pass on your faith to your child.

The Tip of the Week gives quick ideas on ways to deal with the common (and sometimes funny!) trials of everyday life with a young child or shares ideas about simple fun activities your young family can do together successfully.

Use this paper every day of the week to help you pass on God's love to your child in a variety of enjoyable interactive ways that help to reinforce the week's lesson focus and content, remember the week's Scripture and build family relationships as you learn together!

Talking with Young Children: Make Your Words Count!

Imagine that you are standing among giants who constantly mumble words you don't understand. That's a great deal what it's like to be a young child in a crowd of talking adults! Although we may talk at children, we find that unless we know how to talk effectively with them, they seldom hear or respond. We need to talk so that they can understand!

First, follow Jesus' example. Remember that little children need far more action than talk. When Jesus was around little children, He loved them; He didn't lecture them. Actions say more than words ever could. Young children often don't understand the meaning of all our words; our body language, facial expression and tone of voice contain most of the meaning they grasp.

How to Talk Effectively

• First put yourself at the child's eye level. Squat, kneel or sit.

• Look into the child's eyes, not only to get the child's attention, but also to say "You're important to me—I care about you." Smile as you talk. Avoid wearing that pasted-on smile grown-ups sometimes wear around children. Children need to see genuine

love, not a professional manner that wears a professional smile.

• As you converse, show a child the same respect you would show an adult. Don't interrupt, put down or talk down to any child!

• Listen without passing judgment. Young children are in the process of making words work to put across their ideas. They may tell things that they imagine as if they were real. If Sean tells about his dog and you know he has no pets, say, "Sean, I bet you wish you had a dog. What kind of dog do you like?"

• Use the child's name often. A child may well assume you are *not* talking to him or her unless you use the child's name!

• Give a kind touch on the shoulder to express your love as you talk.

• Use these words frequently: "please," "I'm sorry," "that's all right," "thank you."

• Use these phrases often: "I see you . . . ," "I like the way you . . . ," "I need for you to . . . ," "It's time to . . ."

• If you don't understand a child's words, don't pretend you do. Instead, patiently ask the child to tell you again. If you still don't understand, invite another child to listen and help you. If you don't understand at all, say, "I'm sorry. I still can't understand, Ryan. Here. Maybe you could draw me a picture of what you want." Or you could say, "I guess my listening ears aren't working too well today! Let's try again in a minute." Be sure the child knows he or she is important to you, whether or not you understand the words.

• Be quick to see and point out what is good. "I see you sharing with Josiah, Kade. Sharing is a way to obey God's Word. Thank you." You've related the action to

the Bible and helped both children better understand what sharing looks like.

• When a child refuses to cooperate, give a choice. This creates a new focus and puts responsibility for behavior back on the child. "Nathan, it's time to do something else. Would you like to play with blocks or glue pictures at the art table?" Offer choices that are perfectly acceptable to you. Don't offer more than two or three choices. Too many choices can overwhelm a young child.

What to Avoid

• Avoid sarcasm! Young children don't understand it but can feel belittled by a sarcastic tone of voice.

• Don't overexplain. Thirty seconds is about all you can expect for attention, so keep explanations short and to the point.

• Don't exaggerate. Part of your job as an adult is to explain how the world works in clear terms. Don't confuse the child.

• Don't label ("You're a lot of trouble!" "You're a handful!"). Negative words shut down open communication. Correct the behavior with positive directions and without calling the child's value into question.

• Don't correct what you think a child is saying or finish the child's sentence or thought. Young children need your interest and attention as they process the ways to use words.

• Don't use negative nonverbal signals. Sighing, looking away, glancing at your watch or making other impatient gestures tells the child clearly that you are not listening.

Remember that whenever you talk with a child, you can in some way communicate God's love to him or her. Use the opportunity!

Teacher Preparation: Get Prepared to Teach

When we finish a class session, we might say to ourselves, *Whew! Glad I don't have to do anything about this again until next week!* It's a far more common feeling than most of us care to admit! But that attitude can keep us from doing what we need to do most: nurture relationships with young children and involve them in life-changing Bible learning. To do this, a teacher's work needs to be ongoing.

Any person can run into an early childhood classroom, throw a few materials together, keep children from hurting themselves for an hour or so and send them on their way, coloring sheet in hand. But is this effective teaching? The attitude expressed by the adult in the above example says to children: "This is something anyone can do. You kids won't know the difference. You aren't worth preparing for." Since young children so easily absorb an adult's unspoken attitudes, they will soon conclude that indeed this is just another day-care situation where the teachers are nice but where the children are not very important.

Most of us have

an owner's manual for every gadget we own. We seldom read these, assuming that we can figure things out on our own. Sometimes that works. But when it comes to the short and precious time we have to teach God's Word to young children, we need to know the ground rules that will take teaching from humdrum to high-energy!

Prepare yourself. One terrific teacher says, "Begin preparing for the next class session as soon as this session is over. Look at the next session while the manual is still open! When you know what is coming next, you have time to think things through, collect materials you otherwise wouldn't have thought of and can be relaxed instead of harried."

Prepare the Bible content. Don't assume that you know the story. During the week, block out an hour of time during which you will read the Scripture and the teacher's devotional and pray for the children in your class. Familiarize yourself with the age-appropriate version of the story from the lesson. Your goal is to be able to tell it, without being tied to the teacher's guide. Maintaining good eye contact is essential to keeping children involved.

Prepare the environment. Look at your classroom both when children are in it and when it is empty. Ask yourself, *What kinds of clutter collects in this room? Where are the bottlenecks where children can't move freely? What items distract children?* Take time to eliminate clutter, rearrange space and make the room a place that is inviting and involving, not just cluttered. If you share a room, meet with those who share the space to work out ways to keep the room functional and inviting.

Prepare the materials. Ask yourself, *What are some things that might happen if the children have to wait while I collect supplies for this activity? What could result if I don't have materials ready for group time?* It can be very difficult to refocus children's attention when they have waited for an adult to prepare materials. Being prepared is the best way to improve wandering attention!

During the week collect materials and prepare them for the activities you have chosen. Stack materials in the order of use. If your church has a supply room, plan to arrive early enough to gather needed materials before going to your classroom. When you arrive in the classroom, it's easy to place the stacked prepared materials in the area of your classroom where they will be used.

Prepare to arrive early. If you've taken the steps above, you have only some simple setting up to do when you arrive in the classroom. You've eliminated that panicky feeling of needing to do a lot of preparation in a hurry. It's important to remember that no matter what your class's stated starting time, class begins when the first child enters the room. Arriving early to set up materials is well worth your commitment.

One veteran teacher points out that this first 15 minutes or so after you enter the classroom has the most potential for doing the very thing we are called to do as teachers: nurture relationships and involve children in life-changing Bible learning. Children need to be the priority, not our preparations.

Have at least one or two activity centers prepared by the time the first child arrives. This gives even early arrivals a choice of activities. If you still have some setting up to do, make helping you one of the choices you give as a child enters the room. (Yes, this means you must be ready for church half an hour earlier. Commit to it as part of your ministry!)

Prepare ways to interact. We quite often can picture what *we* will be doing during a given part of the class session. But a good question to ask is, What will the children be doing during this time? Know the appropriate ways to talk to young children. Have a couple of backup ideas in mind (a finger play or simple game) in case something you have planned doesn't work well. When children are involved in an activity, it is never time to sneak away to do something else. This is another prime opportunity to build relationships and involve children in understanding God's Word.

Take one more tip from a veteran teacher: We have very little time to impact young children with the good news of God's love. Being prepared makes us ready to do this with a loving, relaxed attitude that reflects His love and care to the children we teach!

Teacher's Role: Ten Commandments for Teachers

 One

Understand that teaching young children is a holy calling of eternal value; pray for each child and ask for loving wisdom as you prepare. (Being prepared says you care.)

 Two

Get down at a child's eye level; show love and welcome by your touch, words and smile. Teach respect by showing respect. (Your actions will teach far more than your words.)

 Three

Make suggestions more often than you give commands; phrase directions positively. (A child must know what he or she can do in place of what he or she cannot do.)

 Four

Be a teacher of great vision: See the most active, the most difficult or the most withdrawn child, not as a problem, but as a person to be loved into God's family. (Remember and repeat often that God loves and has good plans for each one.)

 Five

Give acceptable choices and set reasonable limits; stick to them and keep your word when you make a promise. (Limits foster a child's sense of security.)

Six

Realize that your interaction is always needed, even when children are absorbed in an activity. (Stay nearby to guide conversation: listen, show love and ask open-ended questions to help children understand and apply Bible truths.)

 Seven

Be quick to see, describe and thank a child for right actions. (Describing a child's actions helps the child put meaning to concepts like sharing and kindness.)

 Eight

Remember that young children learn by doing, and provide active ways to learn. (Have several activities ready when the first child arrives, so children may choose.)

 Nine

Know what is typical behavior for young children and guide the child toward desirable behavior. (A young child is not yet able to see how his or her actions affect others.)

 **Ten**

Remember how easily small children absorb our attitudes and how watchful they are of our actions and reactions. (Our attitudes and actions will either affirm—or deny—the truth of our words!)

Transitions: Getting from One Activity to the Next

Transition times are those times when children arrive, leave or move from one activity to another. Quite often, transitions happen when an adult announces, "It is time for . . ." The activity level in the room may increase. Some children become aggressive, some withdraw, and some wander about the room, unsure of what to do next. Teachers may then respond with more directions, louder voices and greater frustration!

Planning for Transition

Transition times need not be chaotic catch-all times. It is unfair to expect children to wait in line for everyone or to sit quietly until the next part of the session gets underway. When we plan transition times as well as we plan the rest of the session, tensions are lowered and learning can take place, even while children are moving through the transition. During transition times, it should be our goal to help children grow in self-control and self-direction.

If transition times are a problem, take time to consider what is causing the problem. Are the times too long? Too short? Is there no activity ready for children who have made the transition quickly? Are there times when teachers seem to disappear? Once you have analyzed your situation, select the signaling techniques below that will best help your children prepare for and enjoy these times. Think of them as "happy breaks," instead of "dreaded chaos"!

Prepare children for what is coming next. Near the end of any activity time, it's impor-

tant to quietly tell them, "It will soon be time (to clean up, to listen to a story, to have a snack)." Avoid making a general announcement across the room. This tends to create a stampede mentality!

Plan adequate time for children to make the transition (pick up toys, wash hands, etc.), so they do not feel rushed. Once the transition has begun, another teacher should be waiting to begin the next part of the session for the children who are ready first. Children should not be punished by having to wait! Beginning another activity also encourages others to finish, so they can join in.

Signaling Transition Times

Finger Play

As young children move from one part of the session to the next, finger play activities can help them make those transitions smoothly. An alert teacher prepared with a simple activity can draw the group together, help them focus on what is coming next

and give them the physical and mental break they need.

Consider repeating the same finger play activity for a series of sessions to signal a particular transition (such as the beginning of circle time). Children love to know what is coming next and they enjoy knowing a finger play activity well enough to repeat it easily. If and when interest seems to lag, introduce a new activity.

Songs

Signal the beginning of a transition time such as cleanup with a song or chant, so everyone can join in as they work together. Songs that include a child's name and tell what he or she is doing will increase children's interest and participation!

Common Transition Times

Entering the Room

When children enter the room, there will be a better (and shorter) transition time if teachers are prepared. One teacher or helper should be available near the door to greet parents and children. Several learning activities should be prepared from which the child may choose. Once a child has been greeted and talked with briefly, he or she need not wait for others to arrive but may go directly into a learning activity.

Using the Restroom

When children need to use the restroom, they should be able to do so whenever they need to. Young children do not have the control to wait! However, if restrooms are not located where children may use them at will, asking children individually if they need to use the restroom during learning activity times or transition times can lower the number of mass exoduses to the bathroom. (Follow your church's guidelines for taking children to the restroom.)

During Group Times

Group times should not be sitting torture for young bodies that need to move! Use finger play and songs to create short transition moments. When children fidget or fight, they are telling you that they need a mental and physical break.

Ending the Session

When the session is over, remember that happy endings help children feel loved and affirmed and eager to return. Use a finger play or a song that says good-bye and reminds children of God's love and care. This gives dismissal a joyful tone. Give each child a special sticker or stamp children's hands for a celebratory feel and simple recognition. One or two teachers should always be available to continue activities that will enrich and reinforce the day's learning (finger play, books, songs, simple games). One or two teachers should be available for the sole task of greeting parents, checking children out and having children's materials ready to go home. (Note: If some or all children will attend another session, carefully plan with other teachers and leaders what children will do during the time of transition, how new arrivals will be integrated into the group and who will lead children in continuing activities.)

Avoiding Problems

• Lines should be avoided wherever possible. It is simply not worth the energy to get children to stand or walk in a line! If children must stand in a line, invite them to imitate the way you are walking (tiptoe, march, slide, walk like a duck or an elephant, etc.).

• Signs can help to minimize interruptions and make for smooth transitions at the door. When there is information all parents need to know, post a sign by the door, rather than trying to tell everyone the same message.

Visual Aids: Making the Most of Posters and Figures!

"Let me see!" is the cry of the preschooler. While we adults function mainly in the realm of words, young children take in information most effectively when they use their senses. Visual aids, or resources, of any kind open another sensory path for a child as he or she listens to a story.

Posters and Pictures

Posters and pictures can effectively draw children to group time as you play question-and-answer games that involve them in searching the picture for shapes, colors, numbers of items, or other details. "If you can see a blue circle in this picture, put your hand on your head." "How many people can you find in this picture who are helping? What is this person doing to help?"

Hold posters and pictures either in front of you or beside your face to maintain eye contact with children and minimize distraction. When you want children to pay attention to you, lay the picture facedown in your lap.

Try posting a picture or poster at eye level on a wall for use as an activity. Invite children in groups of three or four to come close to look at it.

Put a picture inside a large envelope. Slowly pull it out and let children take turns guessing what's happing in it.

Cover a picture with large Post-it Notes. Children take turns removing notes to reveal the picture.

Flannel Figures

Flannel figures should be large, brightly colored and simple enough in design that children can immediately tell what a figure represents. Because they are individual figures, they are easy for a child to focus on and can be moved around to hold interest. For children who often complain of not being able to see, flannel figures can be a good solution.

Flannel figures themselves have many more uses than simply sitting on a flannel board during a story. When cutting out flannel figures, consider covering them with clear Con-Tact paper to increase their durability. This helps adults not to worry about them being torn because children love to use them to retell the story! Flannel figures can also be taped to craft sticks to become impromptu puppets. Additional flannel figures and set pieces (such as hills, clouds, forests or houses) are also easily drawn and cut from backing fabrics such as interfacing or from flannel.

Place the flannel board just above children's eye level. (If children sit on the floor, a low chair may be the best stand.) As you tell a story, use an expressive voice and face. Maintaining eye contact is essential for your expression to be effective! To avoid having to look down or away from children too often, lay out figures in order on a small table or area near the flannel board (or even in your lap or in your Bible), so you will not have to hunt for a figure. Move the figures to reflect the action of the story (walking, moving to talk to another character, etc.) as you tell it.

Retelling the story will be a favorite activity, with children taking turns to place flannel figures on flannel board.

Equal Access

If you want to hold a young audience's attention, it helps for every child to have a front-row seat! If children complain "I can't SEE!" try one of these ideas:

• Lay a masking-tape line in a semicircle at least 2 feet (.6 m) from where you plan to tell a flannelgraph story or show a picture. Instruct children to sit on the line. That way, even if you need to make a second row, children in the front will stay where others can see over or around them.

• Depending on the number of children in your group, bring a small rug or a large beach towel to class. Lay it out at story time. Invite children to sit around the edge of it. (This will take repeated practice with younger ones.) This creates a story space where everyone gives you a little space. With a small group, flannel figures can also be laid on the rug or towel as you tell the story.

Objects

Enhance the "you are there" feel of a story by passing a story-related object for children to touch, see and explore. If a story involves eating, consider serving a snack of that food or a similar food. The more senses you can involve during story time, the greater the learning!

To keep an object moving through the group, assign a helper the job of making sure the item keeps moving. Don't interrupt your story to police the passing of the object. Instruct your helper to tell a child who wants to keep an item, "We will leave this out on the table after the story, if you want to look at it again. Now it is time to pass it to Diego."

Instant Teacher Training

Photocopy these miniposters onto bright paper. Display them in classrooms, hallways and offices as reminders of key points about ministry to young children.

The miniposters can also be made into transparencies for use in teacher training meetings.

Give each child individual attention before negative behavior occurs.

Look for opportunities to connect the child's actions to God's Word.

Give tasks that let children succeed.

Choose words that mean exactly what they say; limit symbolic words.

Emphasize the behavior you desire, not the behavior you don't want.

Children don't wait for you to begin teaching before they begin learning.

Your helpful actions, your gentle voice and your friendly smile can say "I love you."

The young child learns more from who you are than from what you say.

Before the child can be ready to play with ideas, the child must play with materials.

Sing God's Word to plant it deeply in a young child's life.

Young children need friend-ships with their teachers more than they need polished story performances.

Use the child's name often to get and keep the child's attention.

A child's brief attention span gets even briefer in a large group where the child is expected to sit still and listen.

Talk about the ways that you see children putting God's Word into action.

Good discipline

is what you do with and for a child, not what you do to a child.

Every action sends a message that goes beyond words.

Establish a few basic rules phrased in positive words.

Show children the same respect that you would show to adults.

Short specific prayers teach that prayer deals with things of interest to the child.

Welcome to Our Supply Room

1. If you borrow it, please return it.

2. If you spill it, please clean it.

3. If you empty it, please leave a note.

4. If you need help, please ask.

Be a skilled teacher by being a skilled listener.

Index